KARL MARX
FRIEDRICH ENGELS

SELECTED LETTERS
The Personal Correspondence, 1844–1877

KARL MARX
FRIEDRICH ENGELS

SELECTED LETTERS

The Personal Correspondence, 1844–1877

edited by FRITZ J. RADDATZ

translated from the German by Ewald Osers

Little, Brown and Company | Boston Toronto

Contents

Introductory Note

The correspondence between Marx and Engels covers nearly four decades, from 1844 until shortly before Marx's death in 1883. It may confidently be described as one of the most tremendous historical and human documents of the nineteenth century, testimony to a friendship of rare intensity. The correspondence, which takes up nine volumes of 400 to 500 pages each in the collected edition of Marx's and Engels's Works (MEW), has been preserved almost in its entirety; Engels before his death merely destroyed a few excessively intimate letters from his friend. Thus the letters present not only a double portrait of the two philosophers and politicians but also an insight into the circumstances of their lives, the development of their political theory as well as their defeats; a picture of their hardships and of their glory.

The letters reveal the most extraordinary details – such as Marx's incessant financial difficulties which gave rise to his almost peremptory demands to Engels – who supported him throughout his life – to send him money. Whether concerned with emigré gossip, love affairs or adulturous liaisons; whether dealing with deliberate political intrigues, designed to destroy Bakunin, isolate Lassalle or ridicule Liebknecht; whether obsessed with their own domestic troubles – Engels, after all, though unmarried, for a time lived with two women, a circumstance which Marx's very bourgeois-minded wife strongly repudiated; or whether revealing Marx's quite gigantic appetite for reading and his capacity for work, even though most of the time plagued by sickness to the very limits of endurance: there exists no better biographical document of the two men than their letters.

Unfortunately, the letters have been largely disregarded because of their great bulk. In the present selection, based on the MEW, we hope to acquaint a broader readership with this part of Marx's and Engels's work; for these letters are an entirely integral part of that work, no matter whether they are concerned with continuous queries addressed by Marx the scholar to Engels the entrepreneur about market and money laws, or with problems of political organization, such as the First International, Lassalle's General German Workers League (ADAV), and Social Democracy.

The peculiarity mainly of Marx's but largely also of Engels's epistolary style seemed to call for special editorial 'interference'. Both Marx and Engels – without any system or special plan – wrote in a mixture of German, English and French, in the same letter, often in the same sentence. In that original state – occasionally, moreover, interlarded with Latin, Gothic or even Old High German tags, terms or phrases – the letters are practically unreadable. The MEW's way out is to translate each of these foreign-language occlusions in a footnote. In our edition these translations have in all instances been embodied *in* the letter itself.

Most of the letters – rather lengthy on the whole – contain in addition to generally comprehensible passages also a great many which resemble a code; there are allusions to names, dates, events, political or other references, which were clear enough to the initiated correspondent but not to any third party without the most extensive apparatus of annotations. Those passages have not been included in our edition. They are important to the scholar – to whom they are available in the MEW – but they would be an encumbrance for the general reader. The excisions have always been indicated.

Our edition is arranged in strict chronological sequence, with one exception. In order to reveal more clearly the dramatic development of Marx's and Engels's relations with Lassalle, the letters concerning Lassalle have been brought together and commented *en bloc*. Explanatory commentaries – readily identified by their italic type – have also been inserted wherever familiarity with events or circumstances could not automatically be assumed or where certain leaps in the chronology required explanation.

'The Moor' was the way Marx signed himself even in his last letter to Engels in January 1883. It had been his nickname among his friends for several decades, because of his swarthy skin and (right into old age) dark hair and beard. 'General', on the other hand, was a nickname Engels liked to hear applied to himself because ever since his brief episode as a soldier in the Rebellion in Baden he had been interested in all things military and wrote impassioned analyses of wars and battles.

A chronological table and a biographical index of names following the text give information about people and circumstances, for easy reference

Fritz J. Raddatz
Hamburg, April 1980

Translator's Note:

All original English words and phrases – some a little quaint or dated – have been preserved.

The Letters

'This urbane young man surpasses all the old asses in Berlin', was an early contemporary judgement on an essay anonymously published in Switzerland and entitled 'Schelling and Revelation, a Critique of Reaction's Latest Attempt against the Free Philosophy'. The author was thought to be Bakunin. But he was in fact a young German. Shortly after Karl Marx's stay in Berlin in 1842, he had arrived there as a volunteer in the Foot Guard Artillery Regiment. As a guest student without entry qualifications, he had attended Schelling's famous inaugural lecture. Now, as a regular visitor to Lecture Theatre No. 6, not far from his lodgings in Dorotheenstrasse, he was attending Schelling's anti-Hegelian lectures. His name was Friedrich Engels.

Engels regarded these lectures as insults to the sacred memory of Hegel. He saw them as outrageous attacks upon the entire new philosophy – Feuerbach, Strauss, Bauer, Ruge – the very thinkers of whom he was a follower and whom he attempted to defend in his polemical essay against Schelling. After all, Engels himself was a member of the Young Hegelian 'Doctors' Club' in Berlin.

While Engels was still a Young Hegelian, Karl Marx had just left the 'Club' and dissociated himself from its ideas. Indeed Engels, an elegant scion of a wealthy Wuppertal family, which had an angel in its coat of arms, had called on Marx at the editorial office of the Rheinische Zeitung. *It was a frosty encounter between the radically posturing journalist and the editor. Marx was by then working on a theory of political economy and had left the philosophical musings of the Doctors' Club far behind him.*

Not until the summer of 1844, when Engels was returning from England, did the two men meet again in Paris. Those ten days in August marked the beginning of a life-long friendship, of a

5

collaboration embracing several decades, a collaboration probably unique in history. It would be true to say that Engels's loyalty to Marx, the loyalty of a man two and a half years his junior, which lasted beyond the grave, has lent a new dignity to the concept of friendship. The extensive correspondence reveals a relationship that overcame all obstacles and all divides. The first extant letter, dated a few weeks after that Paris encounter of 1844, among other things, reflects the identity of political and theoretical attitudes meanwhile achieved between the two men, a turning away from the Young Hegelians which was eventually crystallized in their first joint essay, The Holy Family, *or the* Critique of Critical Critique.

Barmen, early October 1844

Dear Marx,

You will have wondered why I have not sent word before, and you are entitled to do so. However, I still cannot tell you anything yet about my return. I have been stuck here in Barmen for the last three weeks, amusing myself as well as I may with few friends and a lot of family among whom, fortunately, there are half a dozen pleasant females. There can be no question of working here, the less so as my sister Marie has become engaged to the London Communist Emil Blank, whom Ewerbeck knows, and the house of course is now one damned hustle and bustle. Besides I am well aware that considerable obstacles are being placed in the way of my return to Paris, and that I shall probably have to knock around Germany for six months or a whole year; of course I shall do all I can to avoid this, but you wouldn't believe what petty considerations and superstitious anxieties are being placed in my way.

I spent three days in Cologne and was amazed at the colossal propaganda we have made there. The people are very active, but the lack of a proper support is nevertheless very perceptible. Until the principles have been logically and historically developed from the previous way of looking at things and from past history and portrayed as their necessary continuation in some essays, everything is bound to be a sort of day-dreaming and, for most people, a blind groping about. Afterwards I was in Düsseldorf, where we also have a few good chaps. The people I like best, incidentally, are my lot in Elberfeld, for whom the humane way of looking at things has truly entered into their flesh and blood; these fellows have really begun to revolutionize their family management and invariably read the riot act to their elders whenever they dare treat their servants or workers artistocratically – and that is a great deal in patriarchal Elberfeld. In addition to this clique there is yet another in Elberfeld, which is also very good but a little more confused. In Barmen the Police Commissioner is a Communist. The day before yesterday an old schoolmate and grammar-school teacher, Gustav Wurm, came to see me; he too is heavily infected without ever having come into contact with Communists. If only we could act upon the people directly we should soon be on top – but that is as good as impossible, especially since we who write must keep quiet so as not to be picked up. Otherwise things are very safe here, and little attention is paid to us so long as we keep quiet[. . .].

[. . .]

[. . .] Since my departure the Wuppertal has made more progress in every respect than in the last fifty years. The social tone has become more civilized, participation in politics and the making of opposition is universal, industry has made headlong progress, new parts of the town have been built, whole forests have been exterminated, and the whole lot now stands above rather than below the level of German civilization, whereas a mere four years ago it stood far below – in short, a splendid soil is being prepared here for our principle, and the moment we can set our wild hot-blooded dyers and bleachers into action the Wuppertal will surprise you yet. The workers in any event have for a few years past arrived at the final stage of the old civilization; they are protesting against the old social organization through a rapid increase in crime, robberies and murders. The streets are most unsafe in the evening, the bourgeoisie gets beaten up and stabbed with knives and robbed; and if the proletarians here develop along the same lines as the English ones they will soon realize that this manner of protest against the social order as *individuals* and by violence is useless, and they will protest as *human beings* in their general capacity through communism. If only one could show the fellows the way! But that is impossible.

[. . .]

Now see to it that the material you have collected is soon hurled out into the world. It's damned high time. I too will get down to work with a will and start again this very day. The Germans are all still very vague about the real-life practicability of communism; in order to sweep away this nonsense I'll write a little brochure to the effect that all this has already been realized, and describe in popular terms the practice of communism as it exists in England and America. The thing is going to cost me three days or so and is sure to enlighten the fellows a great deal. That's something I've noticed already in conversation with the local people.

Well then, let's get down to work and get it printed quickly! Give my regards to Ewerbeck, Bakunin, Guerrier and the rest, not forgetting your wife, and write to me soon about everything.[. . .]

Goodbye then, dear Karl, and write really soon. I have not since been so cheerful or in such a human mood as I was during the ten days I spent with you. About the establishment to be established I have not yet had any suitable opportunity for taking any steps.

It is ironic that even in this very first letter Engels urges his friend to complete the essay he has embarked upon. This was a planned 'Critique of Politics and National Economics'; it was never completed in this form and only parts of it have survived — the famous 'Economic and Philosophical Manuscripts of 1844'. Engels was a fast worker himself: his research, mentioned in the letter, about communist settlements in the USA, appeared shortly afterwards. But he was not yet to know that this would be his destiny right through his life: to urge, implore and admonish Marx to complete his work. This first letter thus contains an ever-recurring theme, and after decades of friendship Engels would stand appalled before a mountain of unsorted excerpts, preliminary studies and drafts which his friend had bequeathed to him – the uncompleted Das Kapital. *This pattern was set as early as the autumn of 1844.*

Exactly the same subject – though Marx meanwhile had a publisher's contract for the book, a contract he was never to meet and which was annulled in 1847 – characterizes Engels's third letter.

Barmen, about 20 January 1845

Dear Marx,

[. . .]

One thing that I get a special kick out of is the way communist literature has established itself in Germany, and this is now an accomplished fact. A year ago it began to establish itself outside

Germany in Paris, or really just to emerge, and by now it is well astride the ordinary German. Dailies, weeklies, monthlies and quarterlies and an advancing reserve of heavy guns – all in apple-pie order. It has all happened so damned quickly! Under-cover propaganda has likewise produced some results – each time I get to Cologne, each time I get to a pub here, further progress, new proselytes. The Cologne assembly has worked wonders – one gradually discovers individual communist cliques which have developed quietly on their own and without any direct help from us.[. . .] But what we need more than anything else at the moment is a few major works in order to provide a suitable point of reference for the many half-informed people who are full of goodwill but unable to make it on their own. Hurry up and finish your book on economics, even though you may still be dissatisfied with many aspects, it does not matter, people's minds are ripe, and we must strike while the iron is hot. My English pieces will of course not fail to have their effect – the facts are too striking – but still, I wish my hands were freer to do a number of things that would be more striking and more effective for the present moment and the German bourgeoisie. We theorizing Germans – it's ludicrous but it is a sign of the times and of the dissolution of that German national mess – cannot even proceed to the evolution of our theory and have not even yet been able to publish a critique of all the nonsense. But it's high time now. See to it, therefore, that you are finished *before* April; do as I do, set yourself a time by which you positively *want to be finished*, and make sure the stuff is quickly printed. If you can't get it printed where you are, get it printed in Mannheim, Darmstadt or some such place. But it's got to come out soon.

[. . .]

[. . .] The life I am leading here, let me tell you, is the kind the most splendid Philistine would wish for – a quiet peaceful life and nothing but godliness and respectability. I sit in my room, working, I hardly ever leave the house, I am as solid as a German. If things go on like this I almost fear that the good Lord will overlook my writings and admit me to Heaven. I assure you I am beginning to acquire a good reputation here in Barmen. But I'm getting rather tired of it; I want to get away from here at Easter, probably to Bonn. I have allowed the pleadings of my brother-in-law and the gloomy faces of my two old folk to persuade me once more to try my hand at huckstering and for the past fortnight have worked a

9

little at the office; another thing that induced me to do so was the future prospect of that love affair – but I regretted it even before I started to work: this huckstering is too hideous, Barmen is too hideous, the waste of time is too hideous, and what is particularly hideous is to remain not only a bourgeois but actually a factory owner, a bourgeois actively engaged against the proletariat. A few days in my old man's factory led me once more to realize fully this hideousness which I had begun to overlook. Naturally I had counted on remaining in that huckstering business only as long as it suited me, and then on writing something that runs counter to police regulations in order to sneak across the frontier in a wellbred manner, but I can't stand it even until then. If I did not have to record in my book each day those ghastly stories from English society I believe I would have begun to get into a rut, but that at least has kept my anger on the boil. And although as a communist one may well be outwardly a bourgeois and a filthy businessman so long as one *does not write*, to conduct communist propaganda on a large scale and at the same time engage in filthy business and industry, that's not possible.[. . .]
[. . .]

Yours, F. E.

Barmen, 22 February–7 March 1845

Dear Marx,
[. . .]
Wondrous things are happening here in Elberfeld. We held our third communist meeting yesterday in the biggest hall and leading hostelry of the city. The first 40, the second 130, the third at least 200 strong. All Elberfeld and Barmen, from the financial aristocracy to the small shopkeepers, excepting only the proletariat, were represented. Hess gave a lecture. Poems by Müller, Püttmann and bits of Shelley were read, as well as the article about the existing communist colonies in the *Citizen's Book*.* Afterwards discussion until

---

* In December 1844 Engels published in the *German Citizen's Book for 1845* an anonymous description of Owenite colonies in America, based on accounts in various English newspapers (translator's note).

I am. The thing's got a tremendous pull. No one talks of anything but communism, and new followers come to us every day. Wuppertal communism is a reality, almost indeed a power. You've no idea what a favourable soil we have here. The most stupid, most indolent, the most philistine of people, who were never interested in anything in the world, are beginning to be almost enthusiastic about communism.[...]
[...]

Yours, F. E.

Very typical of Marx's love of polemics was his sudden burst of activity in working on his book against the Young Hegelians, originally intended to be no more than a bit of aggressive fun – the Critique of Critical Critique (The Holy Family). *It had diverted him for months from his work on his book on political economy – and Engels now holds the product in his hands with some measure of bewilderment.*

Barmen, 17 March 1845

Dear Marx,
[...]
The *Critical Critique* – I believe I wrote to you to say it had arrived – is quite splendid. Your examination of the Jewish question, the history of materialism and *mystères* are marvellous and will have excellent effect. Having said all this, the thing is too big. The sovereign contempt which we both display towards *Literatur-Zeitung* sorely contrasts with the 22 printer's sheets which we devote to it. Moreover, the major part of the critique of speculation and of the abstract essence generally will be beyond the comprehension of the broader public and indeed not arouse general interest. But otherwise the whole book is splendidly written – enough to laugh yourself silly. The Bauers won't be able to say a word, and as for Bürgers, provided he advertises it in the first Püttmann issue, he may when the occasion offers mention the reason why I have not discoursed very much and only on such things as could be written without any thorough examination of the matter – my brief ten-day sojourn in Paris. Anyway it looks odd that I have perhaps 1½ sheets

in it and you over 20. As for the reference to 'conditions of the whores', you would have done better to delete that. It is too thin and altogether too insignificant.

[. . .]

Let me tell you I'm leading a real dog's life. What with all the meetings and the 'debauchery' of several of our local communists, whom I naturally meet, the whole religious fanaticism of my old man has been awakened again, further intensified by my declaration that I will definitively give up being a filthy businessman – and my public appearance as a communist has moreover given rise to a splendid bourgeois fanaticism in him. Just picture my position. Since I'm leaving in a fortnight or so I don't wish to start a row; I submit to everything, and that they are not used to and so they grow bolder. When I get a letter it is sniffed at from all sides before I receive it myself. Since they know they are all letters from communists they invariably put on pious long-suffering faces – enough to drive you round the bend. If I leave the house – the same faces. If I stay in my room and work, naturally on communism, they know that – the same faces. I cannot eat, drink, sleep or let out a single fart without those self-same confounded pious faces before my eyes. No matter whether I go out or stay at home, whether I keep silent or speak, whether I read or write, whether I laugh or not, no matter what I do – immediately my old man puts on that infamous mug. At the same time my old man is so stupid that he throws communism and liberalism into the same pot as 'revolutionary' and thus, for example, in spite of all my protestations, keeps holding me responsible for the insanities of the British *bourgeoisie* in parliament! And now the pious season has started at home here anyway. A week ago today two of my siblings were confirmed, today the whole kith and kin are trotting off to Holy Communion – the body of the Lord has done its work, the long faces this morning surpassed everything. To make misfortune complete I spent last night with Hess in Elberfeld, where we learnedly talked communism until 2 am. Needless to say, long faces today about my late return, hints that I was probably in clink. Eventually they summoned the courage to ask where I had been. With Hess. 'With Hess! Good Heavens!' A pause, an intensification of Christian despair in their faces. 'The people you've chosen to consort with!' Sighs, etc. It's enough to drive you insane. You've no idea of the malice of this Christian chase after my 'soul'. All my old man now needs is to discover that *Critical Critique* exists and he may well kick me out of the house. And there is this continuing annoyance of seeing that you just cannot get anywhere with those people, that they positively *want* to torment and torture themselves with their visions of hell, and that one cannot even make them understand the most ordinary principles of fairness. If it weren't for my mother, who has a fine fund of humanity and only lacks all independence *vis-à-vis* my father, and whom I genuinely love, I would not for a moment consider making even the minutest concession to my fanatical and despotic old man. But as it is, my mother worries herself sick every moment of the day and each time she is specifically annoyed with me has a headache for a week – it's just no longer bearable, I've got to get away and I scarcely know how to hang on for these few weeks that I'm still here. But I'll manage somehow.

[. . .]

Yours, E.

Paris, 9 March 1847

Dear Marx,

[. . .]

If it is at all possible do come over here in April. By 7 April I'm moving out – I don't know yet where to – and shall also have some money about that time. We might spend some time boozing together very merrily. As the police are now rather unpleasant (apart from the Saxon I wrote to you about, my old opponent Eisermann has also been harassed – both have remained here, see K. Grün in *Kölner Zeitung*), it will therefore be best to follow Börnstein's advice. Try the French Envoy about getting a passport *for your emigration*; if this doesn't work we'll see what can be done here – there's bound to be some conservative Deputy who might be mobilized sixth-hand. You've got quite simply to leave that annoying Brussels and come to Paris, and I'm also longing to have a few drinks with you. Either a dissolute character or a schoolmaster – that's all one can be here; a dissolute character among dissolute rascals, and that's a very bad role if you've got no money, or a schoolmaster of Ewerbeck, Bernays and associates. Or else allow the chiefs of the French Radicals to give you wise advice which you must subsequently defend against the other asses so they don't strut

about too proudly in their woolly Germanity. If only I had an income of 5,000 fr. I'd do nothing but work and have fun with the women till I was finished. If there weren't any Frenchwomen life wouldn't be worth living at all. But so long as there are *grisettes* – bah! This does not mean that one doesn't enjoy now and again discussing some proper subject or enjoying life with a little refinement, but neither is possible with the gang of my acquaintances. You've got to come here.
[. . .]

Yours, F. E.

The fact that Marx's first extant letter to Engels dates only from the spring of 1847, when he was already in Brussels – i.e. three years after Engels's first letter – is of course fortuitous; earlier ones have no doubt been destroyed. Nevertheless even this detail conveys the correct impression: Engels was invariably the wooing and caring partner.

Yet the fact that this first letter by Marx already contains the two principal themes of the entire correspondence – almost like leitmotifs – is not fortuitous. Sickness and money, the latter often demanded by Marx in a tone of command, were to characterize his letters throughout the next decades.

Brussels, 15 May 1847

Dear Engels!
[. . .]
I am at the moment in such financial straits that I had to take recourse to the drawing of these bills, and those two asses shan't be given something for nothing in the end. In case these asses want to accept the bills only for *appearance's sake* I must of course know this at once.

Since the matter is *most pressing* I expect you not to waste a single day to straighten everything out and *notify me.*

Here in Brussels a buyer-up of bills of exchange has been located.

There's no more to tell you. About 12 days ago Breyer *bled* me, but on the *right* arm instead of the *left*. Since I continued to work as if nothing had happened the wound festered instead of healing up. The matter might have got dangerous and cost me my arm. Now it's as good as healed. But my arm's still weak. Must not be overworked.

Yours, Marx

Meanwhile in Brussels Marx had become a member of the 'League of the Just', had set up a 'Communist Correspondence Bureau', designed to bring together the countless revolutionary groups and associations, and had founded a 'Communist Party', consisting for the moment of seventeen members, all of them Germans. He was chief of the Brussels chapter while Engels was chief of the one in Paris. Marx displayed enormous activity: he travelled to Manchester with Engels, he went to Paris, he journeyed to his rich relations in Holland in order to borrow money, he dispatched Engels to Paris, he received dozens of visitors – emigrés, revolutionaries, democrats. Marx was pursuing a vision: he wanted to turn the 'class-in-itself' into a 'class for itself'; he wanted to make the proletariat aware of itself. 'The head of this emancipation is philosophy, its heart is the proletariat.' His aspiration was a great, tightly disciplined international organization; he was preparing the first world congress of the League in London in June 1847 and the second in December. There he would be instructed to draft the Communist Manifesto. Yet strangely enough, as early as November Engels had such a manifesto ready, with very precise proposals. Today we know that it was Engels who was responsible for the most extensive preliminary work on that text, and that Marx had this preliminary work with him when he travelled to London. The final version was, however, written by Marx alone.

Paris, 23–24 November 1847

Dear Marx,

[. . .]

Do reflect a little about the Creed on Tuesday night. I think we shall do best to leave out the catechism form and entitle the thing: Communist *Manifesto*. Since it must contain a certain amount of history the present form is not at all suitable. I'm bringing along my own version, which I have made, it is simply narrative but shockingly badly edited, in a tearing hurry. I start with: What is communism? And then immediately bring in the proletariat – history of its origin, difference from earlier workers, development of the conflict between proletariat and bourgeoisie, crises, conclusions. In between all kinds of secondary matters and finally the party policy of the Communists to the extent that this belongs before the public. The local version has not yet all been submitted for endorsement but I think that, except for some very small details, I shall get it accepted in such a form that at least it does not contain anything contrary to our views.

[. . .]

This was the famous Communist Manifesto, *the Programme for the Revolution – Engels envisaged it as imminent in March 1848.*

Brussels, 9 March 1848

Dear Marx,

[. . .]

That Cologne business is a nuisance. The 3 best people are in clink. I've spoken to an active participant in the business. They wanted to open the attack, but instead of equipping themselves with weapons, which were easy to get hold of, they went to the City Hall unarmed and let themselves be arrested. It is claimed that the major part of the troops were for them. The business was started unwisely and stupidly; if the reports of those blighters are correct then they could have easily started the attack and it would have been over in 2 hours. But everything was set up terribly stupidly.

Our *old* friends in Cologne seem to have held back rather, although they too had decided to attack. The little d'Ester, Daniels, Bürgers were there for a moment, but left again immediately, although the little Karl Ludwig Johann d'Ester was just then needed in the City Council.

Otherwise the news from Germany is splendid. In Nassau a complete revolution, in Munich the students, painters and workers in full insurrection, in Kassel the revolution just round the corner, in Berlin boundless fear and hesitation, throughout Western Germany freedom of the press and national guard proclaimed; that's enough for a start.

If only that Frederick Wilhelm IV continues to be stubborn! Then all will be won and in a few months we'll have the German revolution. If only he'd cling to his feudal forms! But the devil knows what this moody and crazy individual will do.

In Cologne the entire petty bourgeoisie is in favour of accession to the French Republic; the memories of 1797 predominate at the moment.

[. . .]

Yours, Engels

[. . .]

The Revolution had come. Marx was editor-in-chief of Neue Rheinische Zeitung which under his editorship became the intellectual centre of the Revolution and whose editorial board included, among others, Engels and Freiligrath. Among those published in it was Heinrich Heine. Engels had just visited him.

Paris, 14 January 1848

Dear Marx,

[. . .]

Heine is cracking up. I visited him a fortnight ago: he was in bed, having had a nervous fit. Yesterday he was up but extremely poorly. He is unable to walk three steps at a time, he supports himself on the walls as he shuffles from his armchair to his bed and vice versa. On top of it there's noise in his house, driving him out of his mind, carpentering, hammering, etc. Intellectually he is also somewhat exhausted. Heinzen wanted to see him but was not admitted.

[. . .]

Yours, E.

In the face of countless lawsuits – such as one resulting from the publication of Georg Weerth's 'Life and Adventures of the Renowned Knight Schnapphahnski' – and in spite of great financial difficulties Marx attempted to hold the newspaper like a fortress. Engels wrote to him in a depressed mood:

Barmen, 25 April 1848

Dear Marx,

I've just received the prospectus together with your letter. There is damned little hope of shares from here. Blank, to whom I had written about this before and who is still the best of the lot, has practically become a bourgeois; the others even more so since they've established themselves and come into collision with the workers. The people shy away from any discussion of social questions as if from the plague; they call this seditious activity. I have lavishly dispensed the finest phrases, mobilized all possible diplomacy, but always vacillating answers. I'm now making one last effort, if that fails it'll be the end of everything. In 2–3 days you'll have definite news of the outcome. The thing is, basically, that even these radical bourgeois here see us as their principal enemies in the future and don't want to put any weapons into our hands that we might very soon turn against them.

As for my old man, there's absolutely nothing to be screwed out of him. To him even *Kölner Zeitung* is a pack of subversion, and instead of 1,000 Talers he'd rather address 1,000 grapeshot bullets to us.

[. . .]

Yours, E.

Marx, however, did not give up. He travelled to Vienna and Berlin in order to raise money, and tried to keep the paper going.

Cologne, mid-November 1848

Dear Engels!

[. . .]

I am short of money. I brought back with me 1850 Taler from my journey; 1950 I had received from the Poles. 100 I needed while still on the journey. 1000 Taler I have advanced to *Neue Rheinische*

Zeitung (thereby to you and other refugees). 500 to be paid this very week for the machine. This leaves 350. And all the time I haven't received a single cent from the paper.

As for the editorial position which you all hold, I have (1) immediately announced in the first number that the editorial board remains unchanged, (2) informed those stupid reactionary share-holders that they are at liberty to regard you as no longer belonging to the editorial staff, but that I am at liberty to pay *as much in fees as I choose* and that, therefore, they will gain nothing in terms of money.

It would have been more sensible not to have advanced that large sum to the paper since I have 3–4 press suits hanging round my neck, and may be locked up any day and would then be howling for money like a stag for fresh water. But it was a case of holding the *fort* under all circumstances and not surrendering this political position.

The best thing, once you have straightened out the financial affairs in Lausanne, would be to go to Berne and implement the plan you've indicated. Besides, you can write for whatever you like. Your letters always arrive in good time.

That I might let you down even for a moment is pure fantasy. You will always be my closest friend and I hope to be yours.

K. Marx

Your old man is a swine and we'll write him a swinishly rude letter.

The Revolution was over, crushed. Streams of refugees were pouring all over Europe. Each new country offered security and anxiety at the same time, both hope and disappointment. No one knew yet where he would end up. No one knew how he would live.

Berne, 7–8 January 1849

Dear Marx,

Having recovered from my exertions and adventures during several weeks of sinful living, I now feel a need, first of all, to work again[. . .] and, secondly, a need for money. The latter is the most urgent, and if on receipt of this you have not yet sent me anything then do it at once for I have been without a penny for several days, and you can't get anything on tick in this lousy town.

If only something happened in this lousy Switzerland, something one might write about. But nothing except local muck of the lousiest kind. However, I'll send you a few general articles about it soon. If I have to stay abroad much longer I'll go to Lugano, especially if something begins to happen in Italy, as it looks that it might.

But I keep thinking that I may be able to return soon. This lazy skulking in a foreign country, where one can't do anything useful and stands quite outside the movement, is atrociously unbearable. I'll soon be thinking that it is better to be under detention and investigation in Cologne than to be in free Switzerland. Do write to me: is there no chance at all of my being treated just as favourably as Bürgers, Becker, etc.?

Raveaux is right: even in that decree-governed Prussia one is freer than in free Switzerland. Every Philistine here is both informer and killer at the same time.

[. . .]

Yours, E.

[. . .]

Paris, 7 June 1849

Dear Engels!

I won't write much in this letter. I first want to hear from you whether it has arrived *intact*. I believe that they are again taking delight in opening letters.

There is a royalist reaction here, more shameless than under Guizot, comparable only to that after 1815. Paris is gloomy. In addition, cholera is raging badly. Nevertheless a colossal eruption of the revolutionary volcano has never been closer at hand than it is in Paris now. Details later. I am in touch with the entire revolutionary party and in a few days shall have *all* revolutionary journals at my disposal.

[. . .]

Incidentally, you must see to it that *you raise money for me somewhere*: you know that I have spent the last incoming sums on meeting the obligations of *Neue Rheinische Zeitung*, and in the

present circumstances I can neither lodge and live in total seclusion nor indeed let myself get into financial embarrasment.
[. . .]

M.

Paris, about 1 August 1849
Dear Engels!
I underwent a great deal of anxiety about you and was truly pleased to receive a letter from your hand yesterday.[. . .]
My entire family is here; the government wanted to banish me to Morbihan, the Pontine Marshes of Brittany. So far I have prevented execution. If, however, I am to write to you in greater detail both about my own conditions here and about general conditions, you'll have to send me a more secure address because things here are very spooky.
[. . .]
Freiligrath is still in Cologne. Were it not for my wife's excessively interesting condition I would like to leave Paris as soon as this was financially possible.
[. . .]

Yours, K. M.

The French government wanted to ban Marx from the capital in order to prevent a revolutionary circle from springing up around him. Marx suspected (not incorrectly) that this was due to the intervention of Germany, and saw in the 'offer' to re-settle him in Morbihan a sort of murder plot, because he considered that he would inevitably waste away in the 'bogs' of Morbihan. However in actual fact the Morbihan area is no deadly bog – in this worry of Marx's are combined, as so often, his correct political instinct and a pathetic persecution mania.

Paris, 23 August 1849
Dear Engels!
I have been banished to the Département Morbihan, the Pontine Marshes of Brittany. You'll understand that I won't acquiesce in this disguised attempted murder. I am therefore leaving France.

They won't give me a passport to Switzerland, so I must go to London, and what's more tomorrow. Switzerland will in any case soon be hermetically sealed, and the mice would be trapped at one swoop.

Besides: in London I have a POSITIVE prospect of founding a German journal. Part of the finance is *assured*.

You must therefore come to London at once.[. . .] Anyway what's the point of being in *this* Switzerland, where you cannot do anything?

[. . .]

I'm counting on it *positively*. You *cannot* remain in Switzerland. We'll do business in London.

[. . .]

Yours, K. M.

[. . .]

London, 6 January 1851

Dear Engels!

You will greatly oblige me by sending me the money immediately if possible. My landlady is very poor; she has now not been paid for the second week and is pestering me with frightful vigour.

[. . .]

Yours, K. M.

[. . .]

London, 3 February 1851

Dear Engels!

Are you studying physiology on Mary Burns or elsewhere? In the former case I understand that this is not *Hebrew* and not even *Russian*.

Meanwhile my new income theory has nearly earned me the good conscience that every solid citizen inevitably aspires to. At any rate I am pleased that you are pleased with it. The inverse proposition of soil fertility and human fertility was bound to have a profound effect upon a strong-loined family man, the more so as my marriage is more productive than my trade.

[. . .]

Yours, K. M.

Since 1850 Marx and Engels had been living in England. Marx was in London, without occupation or income, entangled in countless political activities, intrigues, emigré squabbles, tormented by sickness, shortage of money and domestic worries. Engels's situation was fundamentally different. When Engels moved to England in 1850 he was thirty. A police report describes his appearance as follows: 'Age 26 to 28, height 5 ft 6 in., fair hair, wide forehead, fair eyebrows, blue eyes, well proportioned nose and mouth, reddish beard, oval chin, oval face, healthy skin colour, slim figure. Special characteristics: speaks very rapidly and is shortsighted.'

He had now clearly given up the idea of an independent professional activity. He joined the family firm of Ermen & Engels in Manchester, with which he was to remain connected to the end of his life through all kinds of inheritance quarrels, participations and disbursement modifications. He repeatedly complained about the accursed commerce, the irritations and constraints – 'I've now got to be at the office no later than 10 in the morning'. On the other hand they enabled him to lead the life of an elegant gentleman. Engels was certainly a respected member of Manchester society, a member of the exclusive Albert Club, the Manchester Foreign Library and the Manchester Exchange. He owned fine town lodgings, where he served choice wines and champagne to business friends, industrialists, the nobility and the gentry of Manchester. His lodgings indeed were a place 'fit to be shown' even to his father when he visited England. At the same time he had a house outside the city, where he lived his 'true life' with his woman friend Mary Burns and her sister Lizzy. This double life as a compromise with conventional morality did not prevent him from sharing the pleasures of the upper crust, in particular riding to hounds; indeed he kept his own hunter for the purpose. The letters from his early days in England reflect this life very clearly just as they reveal the political isolation of the emigrés.

Manchester, 5 February 1851

Dear Marx,

[...]

A few days ago my old gentleman wrote me an agreeable letter in which he expressed the wish that I should stay here for an indefinite period, i.e. while this tangle with the Ermens continues (that could be till 1854). Myself of course very pleased if he pays me well for my boredom. Of course I don't let on I make this 'sacrifice' to the 'business' and declare myself ready 'to await development of conditions here for the time being'. He is coming over next summer, and I shall then endeavour to make myself so indispensable to him that he must concede everything.

Give my warmest regards to your wife and children.

Yours, F. E.

London, 11 February 1851

Dear Engels!

[...]

[...] I very much like the public, authentic isolation in which we two, you and I, now find ourselves. It is precisely in line with our position and our principles. The system of mutual concessions, of half-measures tolerated for propriety's sake, and the obligation publicly to accept one's share of ridicule in the same party as all those asses – that's over now.

[...]

Yours, K. M.

Manchester, 13 February 1851

Dear Marx,

[...]

At last we have again an opportunity – the first for a long time – to show that we need no popularity, no support from any party of any country, and that our position is totally independent of [...] shabby tricks. Henceforth we are responsible only for ourselves, and when the time comes when the gentlemen have need of us we shall be in a position to dictate our own terms. Until then we shall at least be left in peace. True, there'll be some loneliness – but heaven knows I've suffered that here in Manchester for three months already and got used to it, and what's more as a mere bachelor which, here at any rate, is very boring. Besides, we cannot even really complain that those would-be-giant pygmies are shying away from us; after all, haven't we been acting for however many years as if every Tom, Dick and Harry made up our party although we didn't have a party at all and although the people whom we regarded as belonging to our party, officially at least, though with the reservation of calling them, between ourselves, incorrigible dunces, did not understand even the most elementary aspects of our business? How can people like ourselves who shun official positions like the plague, fit into a 'party'? What use to us, who don't give a damn for popularity, who begin to doubt ourselves the moment we begin to become popular, what use to us is a 'party', i.e. a pack of asses who swear by us because they consider us their likes? I assure you we are losing nothing if we are no longer regarded as the 'correct and adequate expression' of those narrow-minded dogs with whom we have been thrown together over the past few years.

A revolution is a purely natural phenomenon, guided more by physical laws than by the rules which, in ordinary periods, determine the development of society. Or rather, these rules adopt, in revolution, a far more physical character, the material force of necessity emerging more violently. And the moment one presents oneself as the representative of a party one gets swept into that vortex of irresistible elemental necessity. Only by keeping one's independence, by being more revolutionary in *fact* than the others, is it possible to preserve one's independence *vis-à-vis* that vortex at least for a while; eventually, of course, one is swept into it too.

This is the attitude which we can and must adopt during the next business. Not only no official position in the *state* but also, as long as possible, no official position in the *party*, no seat on committees, etc., no responsibility for asses, merciless criticism of everyone, and at the same time that serenity which no amount of conspiracies by dunderheads can take from us. And this we can do. We can always be more revolutionary in fact than the phrase-mongers, because we have learnt something while they have not, because we know what we want while they do not, and because, after what we have seen for the last three years, we shall take it a great deal more coolly than anyone who has an interest in the business.

The main thing for the moment is this: the possibility of getting our things printed – either in a quarterly, where we attack directly and secure our own positions against *persons*, or in fat books, where we do the same without the need even to mention any of those spiders. Either suits me, but in the long run and in view of increasing reaction it seems to me that the chances of the former are diminishing and that the latter will increasingly become the resource that we must grasp for ourselves. What will become of all that gossip and claptrap that the entire emigré mob is now able to put about at your expense once you reply to it with your Economy?

[. . .]

Yours, F. E.

Manchester, 17 March 1851

Dear Marx,

I've had a most annoying attack of influenza which made me incapable of doing anything reasonable or unreasonable, hence my silence. All I could do was send you the Post Office Order last week – you will have received it now. The 5 shillings are for Lenchen who happened to be momentarily absent when I made my exit from your house. If I can at all manage it I'll send you the 2£ for Hip-hip-hooray [Harney] this week or not later than next week, Schramm can take it to him. As I have so far – since I sent you Weerth's letter – not seen anything from you either, I naturally have no further news[. . .].

I am really furious here about the silly arrangements which render any regular and consistent swotting almost entirely impossible to me. One library I cannot get access to, the other, the public one, has only a patchy stock of the things which interest me most at the moment, and the hours are not convenient; which means that all that's left to me is that miserable Athenaeum where one cannot ever get anything and where the library is in the most ghastly muddle. [. . .] From sheer despair I took Cicero's *Letters* and through them I am studying the reign of Louis-Philippe and the corruption of the Directorate. A most entertaining gossip story. That Cicero is really priceless,[. . .]. A more infamous *canaille* than that fellow is not to be found among the ranks of respectable figures since the beginning of the world. I shall make copious excerpts from this amusing little book. No more for today.

Yours, F. Engels

London, 31 March 1851

Dear Engels!

While you are engaged in war history I am conducting a small war in which I am by and by in danger of succumbing and from which neither Napoleon nor even Willich – the communist Cromwell – would have found a way out.

You know that I have to pay 31£ 10 sh. to old Bamberger on 23 March and 10£ to the Jew Stiebel on the 16th, all on current bills or exchange. I first had enquiries made direct with my mother-in-law through Jenny. The answer was that Master Edgar has again been despatched to Mexico with the remainder of *Jenny's* money and that I was unable to squeeze out a *single* centime.

I then wrote to my mother, threatening to draw bills on her and, in the event of non-payment, going to Prussia and letting myself be locked up. I seriously considered this latter course if it came to it, but this resource naturally came to an end the moment those asses in the newspapers began to howl about the workers abandoning me, the decline of my popularity and suchlike. Otherwise the business would have looked too much like a political *coup de théâtre*, like a more or less deliberate imitation of Jesus Christ Kinkel. I'd given my old lady the 20 March as the time limit.

On 10 March she wrote to me that she would write to our relations; on 18 March she wrote that the relations had *not* written back, meaning that the business was at an end. I immediately answered her, saying that I stood by my first letter.

I paid Stiebel his 10£ on 16 March, thanks to Pieper's help. On 23 March, having taken a number of fruitless steps, the bill for old Bamberger naturally had to be protested. I had a ghastly scene with the old chap, who had moreover hideously berated me to the worthy Seiler. That ass had got his banker in Trier to make enquiries about me from the banker Lautz. This fellow, my old man's banker and my personal enemy, naturally wrote the greatest nonsense about me and moreover whipped up my old lady against me.

As for old Bamberger I had no choice but to give him two bills of exchange, one on him for London, 4 weeks after 24 March, the other on my old lady for 3 weeks after Trier, in order to cover the first one. I immediately informed my old lady. Today, simultaneously with your letter, I received one from my old lady, in which she confronts me most *impertinently* and at the same time full of moral indignation, positively declaring that she will protest any bill drawn by me on her.

Thus I shall have to expect the worst from the now enraged old Simon Bamberger on 21 April.

At the same time my wife was delivered on 28 March. The delivery was easy, but now she is in bed very ill, more on social than on physical grounds. Yet I have literally not a farthing in the house, but plenty of bills from small traders, the butcher, the baker and so forth.

In 7–8 days I shall have a copy here of the testament from Scotland. If anything at all can be done with it the little Bamberger will do it, in his own interest. But I cannot rely on it.

You will agree that this general shit is not very pleasant and that I am stuck in this petit-bourgeois muck right up to the tip of my skull. And on top of it all one has exploited the workers! And seeks dictatorship! Frightful!

But this is not all. The manufacturer who lent me money in Brussels, from Trier, is pressing me and demands repayment because his ironworks is in a bad way. So much the worse for him. I cannot cope with that.

But finally, in order to lend the business a tragi-comical twist, there is yet a mysterious affair which I shall now reveal to you in very few words. But I am just being disturbed and have to go to my wife to minister to the patient. That other business then, in which you too play a part, next time.

Yours, K. M.

[. . .]

By the way, how do merchants, manufacturers, etc., calculate that part of their income which they themselves consume? Is that money also collected from the banker or how is it treated? Please answer this question.

Brecht once said that Marx's money-raising operations yielded nothing in energy to those of a small permanently bankrupt principality. In point of fact Marx's financial problems never came to an end, no matter whether £1 came from Engels, or £10 or £100 or, from 1857 onwards regular major payments, or after 1868, a lavish pension. In just the same way 'The Economy' never came to an end, even though this was to be Marx's reply to 'that whole emigré mob'. The promises remained unfulfilled.

London, 2 April 1851

Dear Engels!

Your postal order was most welcome. And this time speed has multiplied the capital by 10 just like the railway revenues of Monsieur Proudhon.

You will realize that I am not idle. And with what you've advanced me I hope to scrape together what is still missing from various corners of the earth.

I will not write to you about the mysterious business because I shall certainly come to you towards the end of April whatever happens. I've got to get away for a week.

The worst is that I am suddenly baulked in my library studies. I've got to the point where I can finish that whole economic shit in 5 weeks. When that's done I shall work on the Economy at home and pick on some other science at the Museum. This is beginning to bore me. Basically this field of learning has not progressed since A. Smith and D. Ricardo, no matter how much has happened in detailed, and often super-refined, investigations.

Answer the question I put to you in my last letter.
[. . .]
My wife has unfortunately given birth to a girl and not to a boy. Worse still, she is very debilitated.
[. . .]

Yours, K. M.

Incidentally I shall be obliged if in the present circumstances you will write as often as possible. You know that my contacts here are more or less confined to stupid oafs.

Manchester, 3 April 1851

Dear Marx,
[. . .]
As for your question in your last but one letter, it is not entirely clear. However, I think the following will do for you. The merchant as a firm, as a profit-maker, and the same merchant as a consumer

are two totally different persons in commerce, persons antagonistic to one another. The merchant as a firm is called capital account or profit-and-loss account. The merchant as a glutton, drunkard, home occupier or offspring-producer is called household expense account. Capital account therefore debits to the household expense account every centime which travels from the commercial into the private pocket, and since the household expense account has only a debit and not a credit, in other words is one of the worst debtors of the firm, the entire debit total of the household expense account is pure loss at the end of the year and is deducted from the profit. In striking the balance and calculating the profit percentage, on the other hand, the sums used for household are normally regarded as still existent, as part of the profit; thus for 100,000 Taler capital, if 10,000 Taler has been earned but 5,000 blown, one calculates that a 10% profit has been made, and when all this has been correctly entered the capital account in the following year figures with a debit of 105,000 Taler. The procedure itself is a little more involved than I have here described, because capital account and household expense account are brought together only rarely or only when the annual balance is struck, and because the household expense account usually figures as debtor to the cash account which acts as the broker – but it comes to the same in the end.

[. . .]

I'm delighted that, in spite of everything, you'll come here at the end of the month. But you must on that occasion bring me the complete copy of *Neue Rheinische Zeitung* – I shall compile from it files on all the German democratic asses and likewise on the French – a task that certainly has to be done before we are catapulted into some mess again. It would be useful if the worthy Liebknecht, who is good enough for this, went to the Museum for that purpose and there looked up the voting figures of the Berlin, the Frankfurt and the Vienna assemblies, which are bound to be there (in the shorthand reports) and if he excerpted from them all those on the Left.

[. . .]

Let me know how your wife is doing and give her my warmest regards.

I am glad you have at last finished the Economy. The thing was really dragging on too much, and as long as you still have before you one single unread book you consider important, you won't get down to the writing.

[. . .]

Yours, F. E.

Manchester, 15 April 1851

Dear Marx,

Enclosed Post Office Order £5.

If your wife's state of health and your other circumstances permit, come here the day after tomorrow, Thursday. You have 3 trains to choose from: (1) at half-past six in the morning, arriving here at 2 o'clock (has 2nd class); (2) the Parliamentary Train at seven in the morning (2nd and 3rd class), arriving at half-past six in the evening; (3) at 12 noon, arrving at 9 in the evening (2nd class). We might then drive about the neighbourhood a little from Friday to Monday. In any case write to me at once whether and by what train you'll come; I shall be at the station. If you cannot come Thursday, although in many respects this would be preferable, come on Friday. In any case let me know at once where and how.

I'll leave everything else for word of mouth and had better go off now to get the postal order. Regards to your wife and children.

Yours, F. E.

The office was again too crowded – enclosed ½ five-pound note – the other half by the next post.

Manchester, 1 May 1851

Dear Marx,

[. . .]

To judge by *The Times* things must be terrible in London now that the Tartars, French, Russians and other barbarians are said to have taken total possession of it. Additionally the prospect of these being joined by brigades of police spies from all continents and even Prussian gendarmes, not counting the German democratic friends à la Otterberg who will come in June to see the great Exhibition and the great men – that'll be a real treat. Watch it, you'll have people with letters of recommendation, or even without anything of the

31

sort, sent to plague you, demanding from you that you should show them Ledru, Mazzini, L. Blanc and Caussidière, and who will afterwards bellyache terribly in Germany because you did not get them an invitation to Feargus O'Connor's luncheon. People will come and say: Herr Marx? Pleased to meet you – you know me, I am Neuhaus, the chief of the Thuringian movement!

[. . .]

                                                              Yours, F. E.

[. . .]

                                            Manchester, 9 May 1851
Dear Marx,

[. . .]

[. . .] Besides, did we not have to fight and capture our position also in 1848 in Cologne, and yet the democratic, red or even communist mob will never *love* us.

[. . .]

                                                              Yours, F. E.

[. . .]

                                        Manchester, about 6 July 1851
Dear Marx,

After having dragged my old man about here for a week I have now happily despatched him again and can at last send you the enclosed Post Office Order for £5 today. By and large I may be well satisfied with the result of my interview with the old gentleman. He needs me here for at least three years, and I have not entered into any obligations for the long term, and not even for the 3 years, nor in fact were they demanded – neither with regard to authorship nor to staying here in the event of a revolution.

He does not even seem to consider revolution, that's how sure the people are now! On the other hand, I started by demanding representation and living expenses – about £200 per annum, and this was agreed without any great difficulty. With such a salary things should be all right, and if everything stays quiet until the next balance sheet, and if the business here does well, then he will have quite a different blood-letting yet – even this year I shall greatly exceed the two hundred pounds. Besides, he let me look into his entire business affairs both here and over there, and since he has done very good business and more than doubled his capital since 1837, it is obvious that I am no more embarrassed than is necessary.

Incidentally the old man is also devious enough. His plan, which however can be implemented only very slowly and with difficulties and which will hardly ever come off because of the wranglings with the Ermens, is to let Peter Ermen move to Liverpool, which he himself wants, and then place the whole management of the local office – where G. Ermen would then run the factory – into my hands. In this way I should then be tied. Of course I protested that surely this was beyond my strength and acted the modest man. Nevertheless, if my old man had stayed a few days longer we should have got into each other's hair; that man can't bear good fortune, he gets cocky, relapses into his old sermonizing and becomes provoking, at the same time he is so stupid and tactless that, e.g., he tried, even on the last day of his stay, to use the presence of one of the Ermens, when he thought me muzzled and relied on my sense of propriety, to score points off me by singing a paean about Prussia's institutions. Needless to say, a few words and a furious glance were enough to send him back within his bounds but it was also enough to put the two of us abruptly back again upon a chillier footing – at the very moment of parting – and I confidently expect that in one way or another he will try to revenge himself for this check. We shall see. Provided the business has no immediate practical disadvantages, i.e. on my financial position, I naturally prefer a cool business relationship to all that sentimental humbug.

[. . .]

Yours, F. E.

Manchester, 17 July 1851

Dear Marx,

[. . .] I'm ready to believe that you are in dire straits and it is all the more annoying to me that until the beginning of next month I shan't have a single centime at my disposal. If you cannot wait that long couldn't you arrange for Weerth to lend you something until then? I can pay back £5 on 1 August and again £5 on 1 September, and that's as safe as cash.

[. . .]

Yours, F. E.

London, 31 July, 1851

Dear Engels!

[. . .]

You will, of course, without further asseveration, believe that I am damned tired of my situation. I have written to America to find out whether it is possible, from here, to operate as correspondents, together with Lupus, for a few dozen journals, because it's impossible to carry on like this.

As for the negotiations with Ebner in Frankfurt, he writes that Cotta will probably take my Economy – a synopsis of which I've sent them – and that, should they not do so, he will find another bookseller. I should have finished at the library long ago. But the interruptions and disturbances are too great, and at home, where everything is always in a state of siege and floods of tears annoy and infuriate me often right through the night, I cannot of course do much. I am sorry for my wife. It is she who is bearing the main pressure, and she is basically right. One's trade should be more productive than one's marriage. Nevertheless you'll remember that I am not very patient by nature and even a little hard, so that now and again my equanimity is lost.

[. . .]

Yours, K. M.

[. . .]

London, 8 August 1851.

Dear Engels!

You will excuse me for not having written before and at the same time confirmed receipt of the 5£. Pressures from without were so great this week that I could not get down to writing. For the moment

I have protected myself against being thrown out of the house by signing a bill to my landlord.

[. . .]

The *New York Tribune* has invited me and Freiligrath to contribute for a fee. This is the most widely read daily in North America. If you could possibly supply me with an article about *German* conditions, written in English, by *Friday morning* (15 August) that would be a splendid start.

[. . .]

Yours, K. Marx

Manchester, 21 August 1851

Dear Marx,

Enclosed you will find an article of sorts. Various circumstances conspired to make it a poor thing. First, I have been unwell since Saturday for a change. Then I lacked all material – this is purely off-the-cuff stuff and reliance on mere memory. Next the shortage of time and doing work to order, almost total ignorance of the paper and its readership, hence no proper plan possible. Finally the impossibility of collating the manuscript of the whole series for comparison, hence the need for a more or less pedantic and systematic beginning in order to avoid repetition in the following articles. All this plus being totally out of practice in writing have made this a very dry affair, and if it has anything to commend it then it is a smoother English which I owe to my habit of almost exclusively speaking and reading English for the past 8 months. In short, you do with it what you like.

[. . .]

Yours, F. E.

London, 25 August 1851

Dear Engels!

First of all my thanks for your article. In spite of all the bad things you said about it it was excellent and has sailed off to New York unchanged. You have hit the tone for the *Tribune* perfectly. As soon as we receive its first issue I'll send it to you, and from then on regularly.

Now I have to despatch to you a whole load of emigré muck, and if you know a farmer in the neighbourhood who needs the guano of these fine birds for manure you'll be in business.
[. . .]

Yours, K. Marx

[. . .]

Manchester, 8 September 1851

Dear Marx,

Tomorrow my brother leaves and I shall then find some peace at last. All this time I have not been alone for a moment, and it was simply impossible to send you the banknote earlier than Saturday, and moreover both halves by the same post since there is only one delivery on Sunday. As there is a risk of theft I'm giving you the details of the note – it was numbered E/X 01780 and dated Leeds, 15 July 1850. If therefore it should not have reached you go to the bank at once and stop payment – this should be early enough. It was a five pound note.

On Friday evening I suddenly received a letter from my old man, informing me that I was spending far too much money and would have to manage on £150. Needless to say I shall not submit to this ridiculous demand, the less so as it was accompanied by the threat that, if necessary, the Ermens will be instructed not to pay me more than that sum. I shall of course write to him at once that I'm not setting foot in the office again but will leave for London immediately the moment he tries to put this infamy into effect. The man is really out of his mind. The whole business is the more ridiculous and distasteful as this matter had long been settled between us here verbally and I have given him absolutely no pretext for his step. I'm planning to put the matter right with the help of my brother and my old lady but shall nevertheless have to cut down a little for the time being since all in all I have already blown £230 here and this total must not increase too much until November, when I shall have been here one year. In any case this new squabble is again very disagreeable and vexes me considerably, especially the infamous manner adopted by my old man. It is true he's not earning as much here this year as last but this is due solely to the bad management of his associates, over whom I have no control.

[. . .]

Yours, F. E.

London, 24 November 1851

Dear Frederic!

You will understand that because of considerable domestic turbulence I can only now write a few lines to you.

[. . .]

I know that you are in straits yourself now and that my attack and raid in November has pushed you in even deeper, at least for this month. Nevertheless I must ask you if you can, if necessary, raise another 2£. The point is that before my departure from London I borrowed 2£ and at the same time declared *in writing* that I would repay *before* December. In any case I ask you to let me know by return whether it is possible or not.

[. . .]

Yours, K. M.

Manchester, 27 November 1851

Dear Marx,

You will have received my few lines of the day before yesterday. If Weerth cannot immediately find the necessary I shall see to it that I settle the matter the day after tomorrow or by Monday at the latest. In the worst case you will surely be able to delay the business till Tuesday.

[. . .]

The main thing is that you must once again make your début before the public with a fat book, preferably with the most harmless of the lot, the History. Germany's mediocre and lousy scribblers realize very well that they would be ruined unless they appeared before the public with some rubbish or other twice or three times a year. It's their perseverance that sees them through; although their books have little or only moderate pull the booksellers eventually

believe them to be great men if they appear a few times in each fair catalogue. That's why it is downright necessary for the spell to be broken which has arisen through your prolonged absence from the German book market and from the subsequent craven fear of the booksellers. Once one or two volumes of instructive, learned, thorough and simultaneously interesting things by you have appeared we'll have a totally different situation and you'll be able to tell the booksellers where they get off if they offer too little.
[. . .]

Yours, F. E.

Despite the domestic hardships, which tended to overshadow the political events, Engels reacted to events in France with a letter which scintillated like a pamphlet. The abolition of the Second Republic and the establishment of the Second Empire under Napoleon III aroused not only Engels's indignation. The thoughts of this letter are also found in Marx's book The 18th Brumaire of Louis Bonaparte, in which he compared the coup d'état of December 1851 with that of 9 November 1799, when Napoleon Bonaparte as First Consul made himself dictator.

Manchester, 3 December 1851
[. . .]
The history of France has entered upon the stage of most perfect comedy. Can one imagine anything more entertaining than this travesty of the 18th Brumaire performed in the midst of peace with malcontent soldiers by the most insignificant man in the whole world without, as far as one can judge at present, any opposition. And how splendidly all the old asses have been caught! The most cunning fox in all France, old Thiers, the shrewdest lawyer of the legal profession, Monsieur Dupin, caught in the trap set for them by the most notorious oaf of the century; caught just as easily as the dour republican virtue of Monsieur Cavaignac and that braggard Changarnier! And to complete the tableau, a rump parliament with Odilon Barrot as the 'Lion of Calbe' [Wilhelm Löwe], and this same Odilon demanding to be arrested in view of such a violation of the Constitution, and unable to get himself dragged off to Vincennes!

The whole business has been deliberately invented for the red Wolff; he alone can henceforth write the history of France. Has ever, anywhere in the world, a coup been made with more foolish proclamations than this? And the ridiculous Napoleonic machinery, the anniversary of the coronation and of Austerlitz, the invocation of the consular constitution and so on – that something of this nature could succeed even for a day surely degrades the French gentlemen to a level of childishness that is without parallel.

Marvellous is the arrest of the vociferous defenders of the system, quite excellent that of little Thiers and of the gallant Changarnier. Marvellous the sitting of the rump parliament in the 10th arrondissement with Monsieur Berryer yelling from the window: Long live the Republic, until eventually the whole lot are arrested and locked up among soldiers in a barrack-square. And then that stupid Napoleon who immediately packs his things in order to move into the Tuileries. If one had toiled for a whole year one could not have invented a more beautiful comedy.

And in the evening, when that stupid Napoleon had at last flung himself upon his longed-for bed in the Tuileries that bonehead must have been even more confused about just where he was. The Consulate without the First Consul! No difficulties at home greater than they had generally been for the past three years, no unusual financial straits, not even in his own pocket, no Coalition at the frontiers, no St Bernard to be crossed, no Marengo to be won! It's enough to drive you to despair. And now no longer even a National Assembly to frustrate the great plans of the misunderstood man; no, for today at least the ass is as free, as unrestrained, as absolute as the old man was on the evening of the 18th Brumaire, so totally unembarrassed that he cannot even help displaying his asininity in every direction. A frightening prospect of lack of opposition!

But the people, the people! The people don't give a damn for this whole business, they take a childish delight in having the vote decreed upon them and will probably use it like a child. What can come out of those ridiculous elections on Sunday week, if indeed they are held! No press, no meetings, state of seige right and left, and on top of it the command to produce a Deputy within a fortnight.

But what's to become of the whole business? 'Adopting the point of view of world history', we see before us a splendid theme for declamation. Thus, e.g.: it will have to be seen whether the

Praetorian Guard of imperial Rome, which was based on the premise of an extensive state with a thorough military organization, a depopulated Italy and the absence of a modern proletariat, is feasible in a geographically concentrated densely populated country such as France which has a numerous industrial proletariat. Or: Louis Napoleon has no party of his own; he has trampled the Orléanists and the Legitimists underfoot, and he must now make a turn to the left. A turn to the left implies an amnesty, an amnesty implies a collision, etc. Or else: the universal vote is the foundation of Louis Napoleon's power, he cannot attack it, and the universal vote is *now* incompatible with Louis Napoleon. And other similar speculative subjects which one might splendidly develop. But after what we witnessed yesterday no importance whatever is to be attached to the people, and it really seems as if old Hegel in his grave were controlling history as the world spirit and as if everything might be run twice with the greatest conscientiousness, once as a great tragedy and the second time as a rotten farce, Caussidière for Danton, L. Blanc for Robespierre, Barthélemy for Saint-Just, Flocon for Carnot, and that prize ass Louis Bonaparte with whatever dozen debt-ridden lieutenants come to hand for the short corporal Napoleon I and his round table of marshals. We certainly seem to have arrived at the 18th Brumaire.

The people of Paris acted with the stupidity of children. This doesn't concern us, they say: whether the President and the Assembly kill one another, that doesn't bother us! But that the army presumes to impose a government upon France, and what a government, surely this does concern us, and the mob will be surprised to discover what kind of universal 'free' vote it is that they are to exercise now 'for the first time since 1804'!

How far the world spirit, who's evidently rather annoyed with mankind, will continue this farce, whether within a year we shall have the Consulate, Empire, Restoration, etc., pass review before us, whether the Napoleonic dynasty will first have to be knocked on the head in the streets of Paris before it becomes impossible in France – the devil knows. But it seems to me that the affair is taking a strangely crazy turn, and that the Philistines are heading for a wondrously strange humiliation.

Even assuming that Louis Napoleon consolidates himself for the moment, surely this kind of nonsense cannot last, even given the deepest possible decline of the French. But what then? There's damned little red to be seen, that much is obvious, and if Monsieur Blanc and Ledru-Rollin packed their bags at lunchtime yesterday they can calmly unpack again today. The thunderous voice of the people is not yet calling them back.

[. . .]

Yours, F. E.

London, 9 December 1851

Dear Frederic,

[. . .]

Well, what am I to tell you about the situation? So much is clear, the proletariat has spared its forces. Bonaparte has been victorious for the moment because during the night he converted the public vote into a secret vote. With the million £stg. stolen from the Bank, in spite of all posthumous declarations by d'Argout, he bought the Army. Will he succeed once more with the coup if the election were to go against him? And will the majority even vote? The Orléans have left for France. It is difficult, indeed, impossible, to make a prognostication in a drama whose hero is Krapülinski. In any case the situation seems to be improved rather than deteriorated by the coup d'état. It will be easier to finish Bonaparte than would have been possible with the National Assembly and its generals. And dictatorship by the National Assembly was just round the corner.

[. . .]

Yours, K. M.

[. . .]

Manchester, 10 December 1851

Dear Marx,

[. . .]

[. . .] The local bourgeois are on the whole too shrewd to believe in anything more than an ephemeral existence of this Napoleonic farce. But what's to become of all that mess? Napoleon will be elected, no question about that, the bourgeoisie has no choice, and who is to verify the ballot papers? Mistakes in addition in favour of the adventurer are rather too tempting, and the whole infamy of the French propertied class, its servile submissiveness after the slightest success, its kowtowing to power, no matter which, have emerged more clearly than ever this time. But how is that ass going to govern? He'll get fewer votes than in 1848, that much is clear, maybe 3 to 3½ million in all; that would already be a dangerous defeat for his credit. Any financial or fiscal reform is impossible (1) for lack of money, (2) because a military dictator can carry one out only in the event of successful foreign wars, when the war pays for the war, whereas in peacetime not only any surplus but a lot more than that has to go into the Army's pockets, (3) because Napoleon is too stupid. So what's left to him? War? Against whom, surely not against Britain? Or plain military despotism which in peacetime must inevitably lead to a new military revolution and give rise to the parties of the National Assembly in the Army itself? Especially if there is a trade depression!

That Louis Napoleon is about to give birth to something 'great' I don't doubt for a moment. But I'm curious to see what nonsense this will be. The development of Napoleonic ideas will soar very high and, when it comes to grief against the most ordinary obstacles, fall flat on its belly.

What emerges very clearly from the whole transaction is that the Reds have resigned, completely resigned. To talk of excuses now for why they did not resist *en masse* would be nonsense. The next few months will show whether the debilitation in France is such that it will take several years of tranquility to enable the Reds to bring off a new 1848. But, on the other hand, where is that tranquillity to come from?

[. . .]

Yours, F. E.

Manchester, 11 December 1851

Dear Marx,

[. . .]

This is the same foul old democratic logic which has gained ground after every defeat of the revolutionary party. The matter, in my opinion, is that if the proletariat did not this time fight on a mass basis it was fully aware of its own debilitation and impotence, and resigned itself fatalistically to the renewed cycle of Republic, Empire, Restoration and new Revolution until such time as, following a few years of hardship under the rule of the greatest possible

order, it will have gathered new strength. I am not saying that this is what will happen, but it seems to me to have been the instinctive underlying view that predominated among the people of Paris on Tuesday and Wednesday and following the restitution of the secret ballot and the subsequent retreat of the bourgeoisie on Friday. It is nonsense to say that this was no opportunity for the people. If the proletariat is going to wait for the government to pose its own question to it, for a collision to take place that would define the conflict more precisely and definitely than in June 1848, then it will have to wait a long time. The last occasion when the question between proletariat and bourgeoisie was posed fairly distinctly was at the time of the electoral law of 1850, and then the people preferred not to do battle. That and the perpetual pointing to 1852 in itself was evidence of slackness, evidence which, except for the event of a trade depression, was sufficient for us to make a rather bad prognostication also for 1852. After the abolition of the universal vote, after the displacement of the proletariat from the official stage, it is surely asking a little too much of the official parties that they should pose the question in a way convenient to the proletariat. And how then was the question posed in February 1848? Then the people were just as unconcerned as now. And there is no denying that, if the revolutionary party begins, amidst a revolutionary development, to allow decisive turning points to pass by without objecting with a single word, or if it intervenes without being victorious, it may, with a high degree of certainty, be regarded as broken for quite a while. Evidence the insurrections following Thermidor and after 1830. And the gentlemen who now proclaim so loudly that the *vrai peuple* is awaiting its opportunity are in danger of gradually joining the same crowd as the impotent Jacobins of 1795–9 and the Republicans of 1831–9 and of looking very foolish.
[...]

Yours, F. E.

London, 27 February 1852

Dear Engels!

[...] In spite of her promise I have so far had no word from my old lady. Likewise I have had no answer to letters to acquaintances in Germany. For a week now I have been at the pleasant stage where, for a lack of coats, stored at the pawnshop, I no longer leave the house and for lack of credit can no longer eat meat. All this is just shit but I am afraid that one day this mess may end in a scandal. The only good news we had was from my ministerial sister-in-law – the news of illness of my wife's indestructible uncle. If that dog dies now I'll be out of trouble.

[. . .]

Yours, K. Marx

Manchester, 18 March 1852

Dear Marx,

[. . .]

[. . .] On top of the article for the *Tribune* and a weekly report to my old man, to have to write now a regular weekly piece for him [Ernest C. Jones] or Weydemeyer is a bit much when one's beavered away all day at the office. Besides I've got to sort out my Slav affairs at long last. In my present amateurish way I haven't got anywhere in a whole year, but seeing that I have made a start and advanced too far to drop the business I really must now devote some time to it regularly. For the past fortnight I've swotted at Russian quite hard and am fairly clear about the grammar now, 2–3 months more will provide me with the necessary vocabulary, and then I can start on something else. I must get the Slav languages finished this year, and basically they aren't all that difficult. Apart from the linguistic interest the matter has for me there is also the consideration that one of us at least should, when it comes to the next great dramatic performance, know the languages, the history, the literature and the details of the social institutions of just those nations with which we shall be instantly in conflict. Bakunin really became somebody only because nobody knew Russian. And that old pan-Slav swindle of transforming ancient Slav common property into communism and portraying the Russian peasants as born communists will again be trotted out a good deal.

[. . .]

Yours, F.E.

[. . .]

London, 14 April 1852

Dear Frederic,

I am writing to you just these two lines to inform you that the little child died at a quarter past 1 o'clock today.

Yours, K. M.

Manchester, 20 April 1852

Dear Marx,

I learned with regret that my anxieties about your little girl were confirmed only too soon. If only there were some means of moving you with your family into a healthier neighbourhood and more spacious accommodation!

I would have gladly sent you some money but I spent so much more in London than my budget that I shall have to lie low even here till the end of this month, and next month I shall have to pay a whole £12 of bills and for books ordered in Germany. But I'll see to it, if it is at all possible, that I get you something immediately at the beginning of May. I wish I had known beforehand how things were in London then I would not have made this basically quite superfluous journey to London and would thus have had a little more elbow-room.

[. . .]

Yours, F. E.

London, 23 April 1852

Dear Frederic!

I went through such a shitty mess last week that you can't even imagine it. On the day of the funeral the promised monies failed to arrive from all sides so that I was eventually compelled to run to some French neighbours in order to pay the English death-hounds. To add to the misfortune, Weydemeyer's letter arrived to the effect that all prospects seem shipwrecked also in America. Cluss, whose letter you'll receive next week, now offers better prospects. Although I have a hard nature all this shit affected me considerably this time.

[. . .]

[...]Yesterday, when one of our acquaintances, who had hitherto found shelter at night with Liebknecht, was thrown out by his landlords and none of us was able to give the poor devil a single penny, I wrote a note to Liebknecht to the effect that you have referred him to Hain for that 1£. Mr Hain seemed a little incredulous and demanded from Liebknecht to see your handwriting first. Send me a few stamps, because I have a pile of stuff to send you.

Yours, K. M.

London, 30 April 1852

Dear Frederic!

[...]

[...]I had given Bangya, for Szemere, a few pen sketches of the great Germans in London. This letter, I don't know how, was read to a German bookseller without my name being mentioned to him. He now asks for 'character portraits' of these gentlemen and, according to Bangya, is ready to pay 25 £stg. for a few printer's sheets. Needless to say anonymously or pseudonymously. Well, what do you think? Strictly speaking, we ought to do that kind of humoresque together. I have a few misgivings. If you think that I should agree to this shit you'll have to make a collection from my letters and whatever other things you have such as might contain bits and pieces for the characterization of those dogs. In any case you would have to send me a few notes on Willich 'in action' and 'in Switzerland'

[...]

Yours, K. M.

[...]

Manchester, 1 May 1852

Dear Marx,

[...]

As for the biographical sketches of the great men that you ask about, strangely enough I've been turning over the idea in my head for some time of preparing a similar kind of alphabetically arranged collection of such biographies, one that could be continued indefinitely and held ready for the great moment of 'striking', when it would have to be suddenly launched on the world. As for the bookseller's offer, £25 is certainly something, but one ought to reflect that in spite of all ano- or pseudonymity everybody will realize which side these arrows are coming from and responsibility will fall upon the two of us. If printed in Germany under the present regime the thing would look like support for reaction, and no amount of firm ideological prefaces could prevent this. And that is always fatal. If the story were limited to just a few, say a dozen, of the best known asses – Kinkel, Hecker, Struve, Willich, Vogt and suchlike, it would be more feasible, and the omission of our own names wouldn't matter much in that case, and the business might be seen as coming straight from the reactionaries. Certainly, if possible, we should do the thing together. Let me know what you think had best be done, and then we'll see. 25 pounds is certainly worth a minor scandal.

[. . .]

Yours, F. E.

Manchester, 19 May 1852

Dear Marx,

Things are progressing well. Tomorrow or the next day my old man leaves again, highly satisfied with his business. The business here will be completely reorganized and continued on a new basis. The increment has been happily captured, and as soon as the contracts are signed and my old man disappears the afore-mentioned banknote will make its appearance at your address. The best thing about it is that I am not signing anything at all; my old man is wise enough not to trust me entirely in political respects and to be very careful therefore lest he be involved in new unpleasantness through me in the future. Moreover, if the need should arise, I can arrange things, observing a few decent appearances, so that I am replaced by one of my brothers, with the result that if I should leave, my old man loses nothing but, possibly, a few illusions, and I shall be the one to make a sacrifice, not he. Write to me at once now how matters stand with your character sketches. The point is that with all the changes here I have, for the moment, been saddled with a fairish pile of work, so that I can scarcely consider much collaboration with you during the next few days, but nevertheless I should be glad to see you here as soon as possible. If therefore you could get these things ready as far as possible with Dronke, so that we can then completely finish them here in a few evenings, that would be useful; I would then, before your arrival, make the necessary excerpts from what papers I have here about the persons concerned (whose names you would have to give me) so that we can progress quickly. It just occurs to me that it would be best if you came at Whitsun, i.e. the Friday before – a week from the day after tomorrow – when there are general holidays here. If the weather is fine we might go to the Isle of Man or somewhere, and if it is bad we'll work here. But make sure you come alone. Dronkius will be very welcome here at a later date, but I have no use for him at the moment and he'll only get in the way of our work.

Incidentally, the main thing about the new arrangement is that as from I July my money not only increases but is also entirely my own, so that not a soul has any right to ask me what I use it for. Further details when we meet.

Yours, F. E.

As the present book attempts to paint a picture of Marx's and Engels's lives from their letters it is important that all aspects should be presented – their struggle, their work, their worries, but also the pleasures they took in play, gossip, minor malice and emigré squabbles. Engels's letters about Eduard Pindar, a Russian emigré temporarily living in England, are such an example, as are also Marx's strange efforts to conceal his poverty from his friend Weerth.

Manchester, 7 September 1852

Dear Marx,

[. . .]

A novel has unrolled here with Pindar. I went to his house recently, I don't know if I mentioned it to you, and there found his mother, a most respectable elderly English lady, and a young lady looking very un-English and whom I therefore thought to be Russian. Last Friday I asked whether that *krasnavitsa* [beautiful woman] was his wife or his sister – neither the one nor the other was his answer. On Monday his mother came to my house: her beloved Eduard had gone, disappeared. I wasn't in but was told and immediately went to see her. I found the worthy mother in tears and was informed as follows: in Petersburg Pindar had fallen madly in love with a Swedish (or Finnish) woman and, it appears, ran away with her after his father's death. He had married her in England – she was the above-mentioned *krasnavitsa*. In London he made the acquaintance of a Frenchwoman – the old lady, who of course makes her out to be as bad as possible, claims she's a former Paris whore and mistress of an English manufacturer of comedies by the name of Taylor. He gave her lessons, and, still waters being deep, starts a liaison with her. His wife discovers the affair (the old lady meanwhile had come over from Kronstadt, bringing money and having made her peace with the Swede), and in order to get Pindar away from the Frenchwoman the whole family moves to Liverpool. But he gets Lorette to come there too, and the Swede, who appears to have a lot of patience and perseverance, discovers it again. Follows a new emigration to Manchester, where the old lady finally settles in and herself buys two houses (she lives on the remnants of the ancient Pindar fortune made in trade with building timber and stoneware but squandered in her hands). However, Pindar gets his Frenchwoman to come here as well – she has been here 3 times for certain, this I know because he regularly borrows money from me on those occasions and afterwards very regularly pays it back. But in order to put an end to the business he ran away with her last Saturday, to Australia as his mother claims but, as seems more likely to me, either to New York or simply to Paris. He drew 190£ which belonged to him from the fortune and took it away with him, but straight away lost £20 in the omnibus (the waiter at the hotel where the Frenchwoman put up believes she pinched it from him). The fellow had plenty of money, his mother kept him in everything, and he had 100£ pocket-money.

The Swedish woman followed him to Liverpool yesterday, I am curious to know what happens next.

The poor devil has been horribly persecuted all his life by that foolish youthful marriage with his Swedish ideal – that's what has always weighed him down. With a little more experience and adroitness he could have kept the Frenchwoman here very pleasantly with his £100, but where is a fellow to gain his experience if he loses his head over a Swede at the age of 21, runs away with her and concludes a bourgeois marriage with her! If the silly ass had only told me about it it could all have been easily arranged. But to get entangled with a Frenchwoman abroad in a second more or less lifelong and certainly serious affair, and to run away with her, what idiocy! She's going to make life hell for him, mark my words! Especially if he has really gone to Australia. And yet his old lady is a frightfully kind-hearted and weak person with whom, God knows, he could have got away with anything. But just as Kinkel seems to see the true essence of every love affair in betrothal, so does Pindar in elopement.

[. . .]

Yours, F. E.

London, 8 September 1852

Dear Engels!

Your letter today dropped into a very disturbed atmosphere.

My wife is ill, little Jenny is ill, little Lene has a kind of nervous fever. I could not and cannot call the doctor because I have no money for medicine. For 8–10 days I have kept the family going on bread and potatoes, and it is even doubtful whether I can get these today. That diet of course was not conducive to health in the present climatic conditions. I've written no articles for Dana because I did not have the penny to go to read newspapers. Incidentally, as soon as you've sent No. XIX I'll send you a letter with my opinion on XX, a summary of this present shit.

When I was with you and you told me you'd be able to obtain for me a somewhat larger sum by the end of August I wrote and told my wife to put her mind at rest. Your letter 3–4 weeks ago indicated that there was not much hope but nevertheless some. Thus I put off all creditors until the beginning of September, who, as you know, are always only paid small fragments. Now the storm is universal.

I have tried everything but in vain. First that dog Weydemeyer cheats me of 15£. I write to Germany to Streit (because he had written to Dronke in Switzerland). The pig doesn't even reply. I turn to Brockhaus and offer him articles for *Gegenwart*, of harmless content. He declined in a very polite letter. Finally throughout last week I've been running around with an Englishman all day long because he wanted to obtain from me the discount for the bills on Dana. In vain.

The best and most desirable thing that could happen would be for my landlady to throw me out of the house. At least I would save the sum of 22 £ then. But I can hardly expect her to be so obliging. Then there are the baker, the milkman, the tea fellow, the greengrocer, and an old butcher's bill. How am I to cope with all this diabolical mess? In the end, during the past 8–10 days I borrowed a few shillings and pence from Knoten, which was the last thing I wanted to do but it was necessary in order not to croak.

You will have observed from my letters that, as usual when I am in it myself and do not just hear about it from afar, I am wading through the shit with great indifference. But what's to be done? My house is a hospital, and the crisis is getting so disruptive that it compels me to give it my all-highest attention. What's to be done? [. . .]

Yours, K. M.

Manchester, 23 September 1852

Dear Marx,

The day before yesterday I sent you the translation and a Post Office Order for a pound. At the beginning of October a few more pounds will follow – that is in 9–10 days. I would like to send you more in one batch because, even if the overall total is the same, this would have the advantage for you of easier planning how to apply it – but my own financial circumstances are in a state of confusion at the moment so that I never know exactly how much I shall need during the month, which means that the pounds become available singly and then the best thing to do is to dispatch them to you at once. Next month I'm going to regulate the affair on a business basis and shall then soon be able to make estimates. [. . .]

Yours, F. E.

[. . .]

London, 28 September 1852

Dear Engels!

You have not received a letter from me for some time. Main reason was Weerth who more or less monopolizes the evenings which I otherwise spend writing. Moreover, not to my excessive delight. You know that I am very fond of Weerth, but it is embarrassing, when one is up to the neck in a mess oneself, to face such a fine gentleman from whom one has to conceal any too-shaming matters. Such a relationship results in double embarrassment, and I hope he leaves for Manchester tomorrow and when he comes back finds me in circumstances which allow me unconstrained contact with him again. Incidentally I think that, apart from my wife's afflicted condition, he has not seen any deeper into my cards.

[. . .]

Yours, K. M.

[. . .]

Manchester, about 1 October 1862

Dear Marx,

Not seen or heard anything of Weerth yet. Why the devil are you embarrassed in front of the fellow? Surely he knows that you've had bad luck for years, and surely from the mere fact that you're still in those old lodgings he knows how things are with you.

[. . .]

In haste,
Yours, F. E.

Manchester, 4 October 1852

Dear Marx,

[. . .] The Pindar novel is taking an entirely bourgeois turn. The poor boy has already got a hangover. Because I have not given him any news of his wife or his mother since *the fifteenth of September* he's bombarding me with letters and threatening to write to them direct for news! The fellow seems to imagine that I spend the whole day there, just as if the Finnish features and the Scandinavian-Germanic heart of his fish-blooded better half were exercising the same magic upon me as erstwhile and still upon him. Master Pindar had risen a little in my eyes by his escape, but these letters again push him far down. He is a Slav through and through, sentimental in frivolity and even in lechery, servile and overbearing; all he has of the Englishman is the exaggerated – as a Russian he's bound to exaggerate it – reticence. More recently the fellow was a little more loquacious, and when the long-closed floodgates eventually opened nothing but foolishness came out. At the same time the besotted Pindar has most evil-smelling desires and discusses nothing with greater pleasure than unnatural discoveries. He is a totally uneducated and at the same time pedantic fellow, he knows absolutely nothing except his few languages; in the field of science, even the most ordinary mathematics, physics and other school subjects, and in particular in the most elementary history he is the purest ignoramus. It is only his stubborn silence that might create the belief that he is educated. He is no more and no less than a little Russian bourgeois with the tastes of the Russian nobility, lazy, dilettantish, soft-hearted, acting blasé and at the same time unfortunately a born schoolmaster. I tried as long as possible to preserve a good opinion of the fellow. But what is one to say of a little man who, having for the first time read a novel by Balzac (what's more the *Cabinet des antiques* and *Père Goriot*), feels infinitely superior to it and talks about it with the greatest contempt as some everyday affair and old hat, while a week after his elopement, writing to his abandoned wife, from London, the (judging by all appearances) quite seriously meant phrases: My dearest Ida, appearances are against me, but believe me, my heart still belongs entirely to you! There's the whole fellow for you. His heart belongs to the Swede, and that's confirmed also by his letters to me, but as for his prick, that he wants to present only to the Frenchwoman. This clash, this Slav-sentimental-mean contradiction, that is just what excites him about the whole affair. The Swede, however, is much cleverer, she tells anyone who wants to hear it that he can do with his heart what he likes so long as he does not carry anything of the flesh out of the home. The fellow, incidentally, has a lack of knowledge of the world and understanding which is in the most ludicrous contrast to the spiritual pretensions that he has as a Russian. He has understood neither the *Manifesto* nor Balzac; that he has proved to me often enough. That he does not know German is a fact, he does not understand the simplest things. I also doubt very much that he knows French. Once the mystery which kept him interesting is gone there's nothing left but a misspent existence. And yet in his letters the fellow tries to continue weaving this long-unveiled mystery – it's ridiculous. You'll see, within 3 months Mr Pindar will be back here and will be a good son, a good husband, a good citizen, more taciturn than ever, continuing to squander the rest of his maternal fortune as before, without making the least effort to embark on anything at all or to swot up anything at all. And such a fellow runs off with an experienced Parisian – she'll make him rue the day.

[. . .]

Yours, F. E.

London, 25 October 1852

Dear Engels!

[. . .]

Dana is behaving very shabbily towards me. I wrote to him about 6 weeks ago and told him exactly how things are with me and that I must have the money for the articles I've sent him *at once*. He has regularly published the articles but not yet sent the money. Of course I have to carry on in the same way regardless. Else I shall again end up as the sufferer.

Now 5 weeks ago I had pacified my landlord with this American prospect. Today the fellow comes here and makes a hideous row to the caretaker woman and me. Today he withdrew – since I resorted to my last means, that is rudeness – with the threat that unless I let him have the money this week he would throw me out into the street and before that, moreover, put a broker into my room.

[. . .]

[. . .] Let me assure you that when I look on my wife's sufferings and my own helplessness I feel like hurling myself into the jaws of the devil.

[. . .]

Yours, K. M.

[. . .]

Added to almost complete isolation in England was remoteness from events in Germany. Marx and Engels had virtually no contacts with British politicians. Engels was deeply hurt that the 'Mecca of Social-

ism', as continental admirers had christened his house, exerted virtually no attraction on the English leaders of the working-class movement.

The advantage which England had to offer as a country for exiles – that it left foreign revolutionaries unmolested – had its roots in just that coolly courteous indifference that might equally become a disadvantage. Mid-nineteenth-century London, with 2,000,000 inhabitants, the capital of a country of barely 20,000,000 inhabitants, was the centre of a gigantic industrial upsurge, a country from where the radical developments beyond the Channel were observed, if anything, with amused detachment. Famous popular leaders such as Garibaldi and Kossuth were publicly cheered but regarded more as romantic or exotic heroes whose heroic words were enjoyed in much the same way as stage thunder – only to be forgotten again. But Marx was in no way famous. Emigrés of his kind were treated with a well-mannered lack of interest. So long as they did not 'attract attention' they were left to do as they pleased – in a vacuum.

All this led, on the one hand, to often hectic attempts to set up, or to found, a separate political organization and, on the other, to a certain contemptuous attitude towards the political groupings in Germany, no matter whether they were followers of Lassalle or of Liebknecht.

London, 10 March 1853

Dear Engels!

Received the £5.

This week I was within a hair's breadth of croaking. It was hepatitis or something very close to it. This is hereditary in my family. My old man died of it. In the 4 years since I've been in England the business hadn't shown up again and seemed to have vanished. However, the crisis is now over and, best of all, without a doctor. But still a little weak.

[. . .]

Yours, K. M.

[. . .]

[. . .] We absolutely must recruit our party anew. Cluss is good. Reinhardt in Paris is keen. Lassalle, in spite of the many 'buts', is hard and energetic. Pieper wouldn't be quite useless if only he had less childish vanity and more community spirit. Imandt and Liebknecht are tough and each of them useful in his way. But all that's no party. [. . .]

Manchester, 11 March 1853

Dear Marx,

[. . .]

It is not very pleasant to hear of the disappearance of our friends. The 'better ones' will come to their senses again at the crucial moment, but it is not pleasant if these citizens embark on the next affair just as wise and no wiser than they emerged from the last. Lassalle, after Cluss, is by far the most useful of them all, especially from the moment when the fortune of Count Hatzfeldt will finally become communal property. He has his whims, but he also has party spirit and ambition, and his little desires on the side and his private affairs, which he will always pursue under public pretexts, are sufficiently well known. As for recruiting, that's a problem, but I think that, as soon as we are back in Germany, we'll find enough talented young chaps who will have eaten, not without benefit, of the forbidden fruit in the meantime. If we had had the means, the way we did before 1848, to make 2–3 years of scholarly and respectable propaganda, with books about no matter what, we should be in a far better position. But that was not possible, and now the storm is brewing already. You ought to finish your Economy, we might later, as soon as we have a paper, print it in weekly instalments, and anything the people do not understand the disciples would explain one way or another but certainly not without effect. Thus all our (by then re-established) associations would have a starting point for discussion.

[. . .]

Yours, F. E.

London, 22–23 March 1853

Dear Engels,

[. . .]

Our people in Germany are really miserable sluggards. Not a word has come from the blighters. They have now read in the papers that a brochure has come out about their affair. But they don't even

inquire. There's no reaction, no drive in those fellows. Old women –
that's all.
[. . .]

Yours, K. M.

[. . .]

London, 8 October 1853

Dear Engels,

First of all I must ask you – if possible – to send me at least a
minimum sum of money at once. 2 weeks ago Spielmann at last paid
up, with a deduction of nearly 2 £. In the meantime of course the
burden of debts had grown so much, the most needful things gone so
completely to the pawnshop, and the family grown so tattered that
not a sou has been in the house for the past 10 days. That Spielmann
cheated me – of that I have now evidence in my hands, but what use
is it? What happened is that the New York firm, at my request,
returned the bill to me together with a letter from which it emerges
that it was *already paid on 22 July*, but I did not receive the money
until the end of September. I now have to draw 24 £ again.[. . .]
[. . .]

Yours, K. M.

London, 23 November 1853

Dear Engels!

[. . .]

Much as your time is occupied I must ask you to send me by
Friday at least – (no need for more) – 2 pages (your usual) and
moreover English so that I don't lose additional time in translating.
The campaign for the winter seems to me to be finished, and
certainly its first period is completed and can therefore be dealt with
in some general outline. I therefore rely on at least 2 pages.
[. . .]

Yours, K. M.

[. . .]

In addition to all other elements the friendship between the two men also included a tentative form of jealousy. Marx was most anxious that no one should emerge to challenge his place in his friend's life, and the slightest suspicion – such as the arrival of their mutual friend, Wolf, called Lupus, in Manchester – gave rise to some thin-lipped letters. Yet this readiness to take jealous offence also reflected the intimate closeness which made Marx turn almost imploringly to his friend at the time of the illness and death of one of his children.

London, about 12 December 1853

Dear Engels!

[. . .]

[. . .] When – this time induced *by yourself* – I touched upon the curious story of the declaration of 'the well-known Herr Dr Dronke' in my last letter I had a feeling that the next result would be that I should not receive a private letter from you for some time until (after 1–2 weeks) grass may be assumed to have grown over the business. That at least is the method which you, since Herr Lupus's arrival in Manchester, have observed with strange consistency in all matters concerning me personally and the two gentlemen. It would therefore be better in order not to reduce our correspondence to mere telegraphy to avoid on both sides all allusions to your friends and protégés up there in future.

Salut.

Yours, K. M.

London, 14 December 1853

Dear Frederic!

You realize that everyone has his moods at some time or other and nihil humani etc. There was of course never any question of 'conspiracy' or such nonsense. You're used to a little jealousy, and the only thing that basically irritates me is that we can't be together now and work together and laugh, while those 'protégés' have you comfortably near them.

[. . .]

Yours, K. M.

London, 3 May 1854

Dear Frederic,

[...]

I should be very glad to get some supplies for *Tribune* from you now since I'm extremely busy with swotting up the history of the neo-Hellenic empire complete with King Otto, but can only present the result in two weeks in, possibly, a series of articles. The *Metaxas* who was Hellenic Minister in Constantinople and there engaged in conspiracies – the Paris *Presse* has an entertaining account of this Russian-Greek Bangyanade – was the main tool of the infamous Kapodistrias.

In my spare time I now do Spanish. Started with Calderón, from whose *Magico prodigioso* – the Catholic Faust – Goethe used not only individual passages but entire structures for his *Faust*. Then – a terrible thing to say – read in Spanish what would have been impossible in French, *Atala* and *René* by Chateaubriand and some stuff by Bernadin de St Pierre. Now in the middle of *Don Quixote*. I find that with Spanish one needs the dictionary more than with Italian, at first.

Archivio triennale delle cose d'Italia dall' avvenimento di Pio IX all' abbandono di Venezia etc. came into my hands by chance. The best I ever read from the Italian revolutionary party. Consists of a compilation of secret and public documents, intercepted letters, etc. Nicely put together. Palmistone (as Thiers pronounces Palmerston) one of the main actors here too. That fellow was ubiquitous in his machinations and certainly led a most entertaining life.

[...]

Yours, K. M.

London, 22 May 1854

Dear Engels,

[...]

I'm relying on you to do the American service for me *this very week* since I am still totally incapable of writing and have already lost £6 because of this sh—, which is very bitter. I expect a few lines from you in the meantime.

[...]

Yours, K. M.

London, 3 June 1854

Dear Frederic!

Now that I am once more on top and the children again all out of bed, though not yet out of the house, my wife is very run down, probably as a result of night vigils and sickbed attendance, and the worst of it is that she does not want to consult the doctor but administers medicines to herself – under the pretext that 2 years ago during a similar indisposition Freund's medicines made her even more sick. Unless the business improves I shall intervene forcibly. In consequence I am unable to correspond on Tuesdays because *that* day Pieper, because of his lessons, cannot serve me in the role of secretary and my wife cannot be plagued with writing in her present condition. As you see I've become a real Peter Schlemihl.* Yet the entire household was, on the whole, very well for many years and I hope will be so again once this crisis is overcome. Basically it's a good thing that the entire household has passed through this business, one by one.

[...]

Yours, K. M.

Manchester, 10 June 1854

Dear Marx,

I was very sorry not to have been able to send you an article by Tuesday's post but it was *quite impossible* because of the lot of office work that now absolutely prevents me from doing articles for you on Monday or Thursday. What's more, I now live nearly three quarters of an hour from the post so that it is too late in the evening to catch the second collection. In consequence I must work Saturday or Wednesday evening. Tomorrow I shall send you a *thoroughgoing* article about the siege of Silistria that should cause a sensation; maybe also a few notes about the ridiculous naval jokes of Napier and on army conditions in Bulgaria.

[...]

Yours, F. E.

[...]

* A character in a novella by Chamisso (1814), who sells his shadow in exchange for limitless wealth (editor's note).

London, 21 June 1854

Dear Engels,

[. . .]

You'll see from the enclosed letter that I am up to my ears in trouble. During my wife's illness, in the midst of a crisis, the good Dr Freund *stays away* and sends me a bill for 26£, desiring to arrive at a 'clear understanding' concerning his 'medical relationship' with me. As my wife's condition was dangerous – and still gives rise to concern – I was of course forced to capitulate to the dear Freund and to promise him in writing that I would pay 8£ at the end of the month and the rest every 6 weeks. If the fellow had not attacked me so unexpectedly he would not have caught me by surprise in this way. But what was I to do? With any other reputable doctor I would have had to pay there and then for the visits and besides, even when that is possible, one cannot change doctors in the middle of an illness as one does shirts without having informed oneself on their ability, etc. beforehand.

I am therefore in a dilemma. I know that you too are in straits. Do you think that I might get an advance of a few pounds, say from Dronke, on the quota due at the end of this month? The last time he was here he indicated that he was prepared to help in major crises. However I'd like to know what you think first. I certainly must pay the first instalment to that fellow on the date agreed, and my bill of exchange for the last few months is already drawn, naturally spent, since I had to pay £12 on the household and the amount of the sum was greatly reduced by articles not written, and besides the pharmacy alone swallowed up a considerable budget this time.

At the end of this week, when my wife feels strong enough, she will spend 2 weeks at Mr Seiler's villa in Edmonton with the children and Lenchen. Perhaps the country air will restore her sufficiently to be able to travel to Trier.

I can assure you that these last few small troubles have made me a very morose fellow.

Happy the man who has no family.

Farewell and remain devoted to me.

Yours, K. M.

London, 13 September 1854

Dear Engels,

[. . .]

Incidentally, as for the 'national budget' *in general*, I have narrowed down the total debts to under £50, that is roughly 30£ less than they were at the beginning of this year. This will show you that great financial artistry has been applied. If negotiations which I have entered into with Lassalle succeed and he lends me 30£ and you the rest, I would at long last stand on two feet again and alter the entire domestic arrangements, whereas now – have to pay 25% at the pawnshop alone and because of the arrears can never get straight. As for my old lady, there is nothing to be done, as has again been confirmed in Trier, until I get onto her back direct.

At the moment being so totally denuded of money is all the more distasteful – apart from the fact that family wants do not cease for a moment – as Soho is the chosen district of cholera, with the mob croaking right and left (e.g. in Broad Street 3 persons on average per house) and it is best to resist that shit of 'victuals'.

That's all for now. I'm sending the letter to your private address because strange complications might play just this by no means edifying epistle into the wrong hands at your office.

[. . .]

Yours, K. M.

London, 10 October 1854

Dear Engels!

[. . .]

As you know, Liebknecht was fluctuating most melancholically between an Englishwoman who wanted to marry him and a German woman in Germany whom he wanted to marry – now at last the German has thrown herself at his head and he has married her, in church and in bourgeois style. It seems that both are in very woeful mood. His job is packing up because the people are moving away. His honeymoon, celebrated at No. 14 Church Street, in a house to which he is mortgaged, is thus made rather bitter. But then, who forced the silly ass, aware as he was of all these circumstances, to get married and just now? Since the person had already in the meantime got engaged in Germany the case surely was in no way urgent.

[...]

Yours, K. M.

Marx's and Engels's relationship with Ferdinand Lassalle – as Franz Mehring pointed out in his biography of Marx – was one of the most complicated in the lives of the two men. It was dictated by love-hate, by political as well as personal jealousy on Marx's part of the man who had everything that he himself was denied: a brilliant part in the social life of Germany, money, and finally a political organization founded by him. Lassalle's fame, not too far removed from notoriety, was based principally on his lawsuit for Countess Hatzfeldt, whose divorce he accomplished in a spectacular and largely semi-legal manner. After her divorce the Countess was a wealthy woman and Lassalle lived with her, participating in that wealth, eventually indeed in the form of a pension granted to him. These private matters, as the letters reveal, played an equally decisive part in Marx's and Engels's judgement of Lassalle as did Lassalle's foundation of the All-gemeiner Deutscher Arbeiterverein, the General German Workers' Association, the first great German working-class organization. Lassalle's every political measure and move was suspiciously watched and judged (usually condemned) in London. The same happened with Lassalle's pamphlets – almost without exception. On the other hand, Marx was obliged to Lassalle in a variety of ways: he used him and readily and frequently called upon his extensive connections, among other things also in order to find a publisher for Das Kapital. The contrast between the uninfluential theoretician and emigré in London and the popular independent politician was striking. Lassalle rapidly advanced from success to success. In the autumn of 1854 he even helped to bring about a settlement between Countess Hatzfeldt and her husband. She was now a rich woman; Lassalle himself was a wealthy man thanks to an annuity for life. He was able to travel, whether to Paris or to the Orient. Marx was suspicious and even furious. He was only too ready to believe rumours to the effect that the Düsseldorf workers had complained about the grand lifestyle at the Hatzfeldt villa; a report by one of Lassalle's collaborators by name of

Gustav Lewy – subsequently even treasurer of the General German Workers' Association – was welcomed unverified as a message from the 'Achtblättler' (workers). Consider the contrast: at the same time as this was going on, Marx was arrested in London while taking the valuable silver which was his wife's family heirloom to the pawnshop, for it was not found credible that the stranger with the wild dishevelled black beard actually owned this 400-year-old silver bearing the monogram of one of the noblest German families. He used Lewy, who had no instructions from anyone but was irritated about having been refused a loan by Lassalle; he also used some obscure 'Colonel Touroute', who likewise fantasized about the profligate life of Lassalle and the Countess at the aristocratic home. Marx would acknowledge whatever suited him. He would take pleasure in reading complaints about Lassalle's 'industrial knighthood' or 'vassalage to a skirt'. But he did not like the fact that this very house of luxury and extravagance was being hailed in solemn addresses, by those same Düsseldorf workers, as the reliable refuge of the most fearless and resolute party assistance. Nor was he pleased that the still highly esteemed fugitive member of the Neue Rheinische Zeitung *staff, Eduard von Müller-Tellering, had found secret asylum there.*

This was the beginning of the phase in the relations between the two men that was to continue until Lassalle's death – a phase of insincerity and double-dealing which even Franz Mehring calls 'embarrassing'.

Apart from a few essays and articles Marx had so far published nothing. The contract concluded as early as February 1845 with the publisher Leske about a work entitled 'Critique of Politics and National Economy' remained unfulfilled except for the substantial advance of 1,500 francs; the book did not exist. The important 'Theses on Feuerbach' were entered in a notebook. His overdimensioned attack on Bruno Bauer, The Holy Family or Critique of Critical Critique *had remained so unnoticed that his next book,* The German Ideology *found no publisher. That political and stylistic masterpiece, the* Communist Manifesto, *was largely unknown, no more than a party 'circular', without public effect. There were all kinds of emigré squabbles and pamphlets, of no real interest to anybody. The American articles, most of them written by Engels, were not known to a single soul in Germany. What would, many years later, be the complaint of German politicians – whether Bebel, Liebknecht or Bernstein – that 'the two old ones' were totally cut off from the German scene, could already be observed in its beginnings.*

Lassalle's writings, by way of contrast, were appearing in huge editions. His activities were on everybody's lips. No matter what he did, his petition for sojourn in Berlin, his expulsion, his publications – everything was public property. And the worst of it was that Marx needed him: 'I have asked Lassalle whether he could find for me some literary business in Germany because with regard to my diminished income and increased expenditure I've got to tackle this seriously.' Lassalle was to set a journalistic plan in action through his cousin Friedländer; it came to nothing. It is worth noting that Lassalle continued persistently to try to help Marx, though this merely aroused suspicion on Marx's part. A later proposal, again through the mediation of that cousin, that he should write for Wiener Presse *was not taken up by Marx, though admittedly for plausible political reasons – the paper's pro-British line did not suit him. When Lassalle announced a two-volume work on Heraclitus, an early study which he had interrupted because of the Hatzfeldt lawsuit, Marx could contain himself no longer. It was now nearly 10 years –since* The 18th Brumaire *– that anything of his had been printed. As for his work on economic matters, the thing which everyone was waiting for, nothing had been printed since the pre-1848 period, since his anti-Proudhon pamphlet* The Poverty of Philosophy. *The announcement of the Heraclitus book produced only wrath, also on Engel's part, and fury and regret that the denunciations had not stood up to examination at all. In a letter in which for the first time he used the intimate address 'Dearest Moor' he said dismissively:*

> *Enclosed I'm returning Lassalle's letter. From firtht to latht the thtupid Yid. I can just about imagine the stuff he's scribbled – including that thing that will prove a 'spark' and that he's so mysterious about. Of course we know that there's nothing to the blighter but it's difficult to find positive grounds for breaking with him, especially as nothing more has been heard from the Düsseldorf workers.*

Marx sensed instantly what this was all about – that Lassalle had in fact written up an old book in order to 'take off' towards new reflections, towards economic theory. Vengeance and retribution were already being sworn on something as yet unknown. The extent to which Marx was upset was reflected even in the vocabulary – from now on Lassalle is 'that blighter', 'the Jewboy', 'Clever Itzig', 'Baron Itzig', 'an utterly vile rogue', 'that pig', 'a pompous ape', 'Clever Ephraim'.

Marx believed it to be a lie that Lassalle started on that book as early as 1846 but at the same time considered it entirely 'old Hegelian', and thus dating back to that period after all, he even fumed about the postage due on receiving the book, which 'has assured it of a bad reception', as though this were Lassalle's fault. Long before Marx even held the book in his hands he had already mocked the 'comical vanity of the fellow who wants to become famous at all costs and who, for no reason at all writes 75 printer's sheets on Greek philosophy'. Now 'the philosophy of Heraclitus the Obscure of Ephesus', which according to Lassalle's offensively boastful remarks was making the scholarly world of Berlin sit up, had arrived. Marx 'dips into the stuff' and pounced on it, but in letters to Engels, and by no means in those to Lassalle; on the contrary. While ridiculing the 'silly concoction' and the 'exhibition of enormous erudition', while therefore leaving not one good hair upon the head of 'the little Yid Braun's' Heraclitus the Obscure, Marx writes to that selfsame man: 'I studied your Heraclitus while I was sick and find the reconstruction of the system from its scattered remains masterly, just as much as the acuteness of the polemic appeals to me.'

That same day he wrote to Engels: 'I have at last written to Lassalle. You must give me absolution for the eulogies that I had to make about "Hercl. t. Obscure".'

It is a similar case to that of Ferdinand Freiligrath, only a lot weightier: for Lassalle had himself announced that he was working on a book on the national economy – he was hoping to complete it by the middle of the following year. Lassalle knew just as well as Marx did that politics were no longer thinkable without economics. But the nonchalance, the impertinence of it! Surely the world was expecting this work from him, Karl Marx; and now this man comes along, a man seven years his junior, a man who has everything that Marx lacks – fame, money, political influence, a social position – and almost casually announces his brazen entry into Marx's inner sanctum. The insult was intolerable.

For at that very time Marx believed that he had got his own economic essays ready for publication. And Lassalle knew that. No, he not only knew it but he had in fact been asked by Marx to find a publisher for it. This is what the letter to Engels of 22 December 1857 alludes to when it mentions the fellow who might be useful in finding booksellers, a letter full of mistrust and threats against a possible rival whom, exactly eight weeks later, he asked for the following mediation: 'You would of course oblige me by seeing if you can find an entrepreneur in Berlin.'

Lassalle found a publisher. Franz Duncker was ready to sign a contract, he was ready to publish the work in separate issues (because in fact Marx had no manuscript ready), and he was prepared to pay an exceptional fee. The curly-headed Jew, the little man from Poland, with the lousy repugnant appearance, had delivered the goods. With relief Marx writes to Weydemeyer: 'Only by Lassalle's extraordinary zeal and persuasiveness was Duncker persuaded to take this step.'

A year passed. The contract dates from March 1858, the manuscript of the first instalment went to Berlin in February 1859 – but it was now expected to be set and printed and distributed at once. Marx was outraged that the publisher, whom he himself had kept waiting for the manuscript throughout a year, should now get down to time-consuming corrections. There could be but one explanation, one explanation alone: an agent, a saboteur was at work. Lassalle! Throughout his life Marx was well-nigh obsessed by the idea of rancune, *of treason, of intrigue. The reverse of that contemptuousness, superciliousness and cynicism with which he invariably judged all persons of his environment and his political relations was his fear of falling victim to secret machinations. But he could see through them all – or rather: he saw them where they did not exist. This was not merely the suspicion of the 'elect', whose Promethean task was to be rendered impossible by inferior persons – inferior both morally and intellectually. It was a mistrustful egocentric irritability against which – close as it was to tearful self-pity – his father, terrified, had always warned him. This was the hour of birth of the 'hired provocateur', of the 'agent'.*

It is therefore perfectly evident now that a new embargo of a fortnight has been placed on my piece in order to make room for Herr Lass(alle). What work remained to be done to my piece could not have taken more than 3 hours' time at the most. But that accursed vain fool gave orders for the embargo lest the attention of the public be divided. And Duncker, that swine, is as pleased as punch at having a new pretext for postponing payment of my fee. I won't forget this prank of the little Yid. The haste in which his muck was printed shows that he is the main cause of the delay of our things. Yet that pig is so much in love with his exudations that he considers it a matter of course that I am positively consumed with curiousity to see his *'anonymous work' and that I have sufficient 'objectivity' to regard the killing of my own piece as quite in order.*

Final evidence: Lassalle was staying at Duncker's house. This circumstance was reported with the same concerned satisfaction as an attack on Lassalle during which he was beaten up with his own stick – 'a relic purchased in Paris, Robespierre's walking stick!' 'That blighter is going to hire a man to slap his face once a year just so that people might talk about him when his own Jewish impertinence no longer achieves this. Meanwhile he preserves a brilliant talent for being beaten up and chucked out.' But precisely four weeks earlier Marx had written to Lassalle: 'I thank you for your efforts with Duncker.'

However, no more manuscripts arrived. Lassalle enquired, and Marx promised Issue 2 for December. It failed to arrive. Lassalle enquired, and Marx promised it for 1860, then for 1861. Marx wanted another publisher, so Lassalle provided Brockhaus. But Marx still had no manuscript. Even Engels's continuous queries of 'How is the book getting on?' remained unanswered. Twenty-two years after the contract with Leske the first volume of Das Kapital *was finally published. The* Critique of Political Economy, *that first issue published by Duncker, was not continued in that form. Marx's main reason was the misery of his own daily circumstances: his liver disease, cholera, and shortage of money, about which – in that famous letter to Engels, when he 'requests' him to be good enough to send the postage because otherwise he cannot post the manuscript – he says: 'I do not believe that "money" has ever been written about amidst such a shortage of money.'*

In order to let this particularly complicated relationship, a relationship not free from intrigue, emerge more clearly the otherwise chronological arrangement of this book is here set aside and the essential correspondence brought together.

London, 2 December 1854

Dear Engels!

[. . .]

I had asked Lassalle whether he could find me some literary business in Germany because in view of my diminished income and increased expenditure I've got to tackle this seriously. Lassalle has now made me the following proposition on which I ask your *con-*

sidered judgement. His cousin Dr *M. Friedländer* becomes proprietor of *Neue Oder-Zeitung* at the beginning of this month but in Co. with *Stein and Elsner.* I am to be the paper's London correspondent. Friedländer thinks he will not initially be able to pay more than 20 Taler per month. But Lassalle thinks he might push him up to 30. That is the proposition. The sum is pitiful. On the other hand, that little bit of correspondence for a German backwoods paper is not worth a lot either. Certainly 40 to 50 £ would always be useful. But the main snag – *Elsner and Stein*! This should be considered the more carefully as these gentlemen are not Conservatives but actually *Liberals* and are therefore more opposed to us than *Neue Preussische Zeitung.* That is the question. Consider it carefully.
[. . .]

Yours, K. M.

[. . .]

London, 5 March 1856

Dear Frederic,
[. . .]

Levy. Sent here by the Düsseldorf workers with *dual* instructions. (1) *Denunciation of Lassalle.* And I believe, after *very close* examination, that *they are right.* Lassalle totally transformed since the Countess received her 300,000 Taler; deliberately repudiating the workers, a sybarite, flirting with the Blues. They also accuse him of constantly exploiting the party for his *private mess* and of having even tried to use the workers for his own *private offences* in the interest of his lawsuit.[. . .] Not his *juridical* acumen but a perfectly common intrigue brought about the abrupt end of the suit. Lassalle did not pay the 10,000 Taler to Stockum, and the workers are rightly saying that such a breach of faith could be excused only if he handed the monies over to the party instead of fraudulently acquiring them for the Countess. They recount a mass of private infamies which I cannot reproduce because each one makes me forget another. Among other things: Lassalle gambled in foreign government bonds with the Düsseldorf man Scheuer who advanced him the money for it. They lost. Scheuer meanwhile has gone bankrupt. Lassalle wins the lawsuit. Scheuer demands the money he had advanced Lassalle. But he sneeringly refers him to some Article 6 of the Code which prohibits gambling on foreign exchanges. The workers are saying they allowed Lassalle to get away with it all under the pretext that he was involved in the lawsuit on a point of honour. Now that he has won, they are saying, instead of getting the Countess to pay him for his work and making himself independent, he is living shamefully under her yoke as a kept man, without any attempt at justification. He had always boasted about what he wanted to do once he had won the suit. He was now deliberately and provocatively casting the workers aside as superfluous tools. He had still attended a (private) meeting, on New Year's Day because a French colonel had been present. To everyone's surprise he had, in front of 60 workers, spoken of nothing but the 'struggle of civilization against barbarism', the western powers against Russia. It had been his plan to go to Berlin to play the great gentleman there and to open a salon. On his return from there he had promised the Countess in Levy's presence to create 'for her a court of literary people'. He had, likewise in Levy's presence, continually voiced his 'dictatorial aspirations' (he appears to regard himself quite differently from the way we regard him; he considers himself to be a world conqueror because he has been ruthless in a private intrigue – as if a truly great person would sacrifice 10 years to such a bagatelle), etc., etc. And, incidentally, quite dangerous: in order to smuggle a man of the Workers' Party into the police as a sham spy he had *given him one of my letters*, which, in order thereby to legitimate himself, he was to say he had stolen. The workers are also saying that given his diplomatic manner he would not have acted against them so brusquely if it were not his outright intention to go over to the bourgeois party. At the same time he had sufficient confidence in his influence to talk them into anything at the moment of an insurrection by climbing onto a table, haranguing the masses, etc. So great, Levy says, is the hatred of him that, no matter what we decide, the workers would massacre him if, at the moment when things start to move, he were in Düsseldorf. They are moreover convinced that when the time came he would make other arrangements in case he got wind of anything suspicious.

All this is just detail, picked out from what I was told and jotted down in outline. The *whole thing* made a *definite* impression on me and Freiligrath, much as I was predisposed in Lassalle's favour and suspicious of workers' gossip. I told Levy that it was of course impossible to come to a conclusion on the strength of the report from just one side; that suspicion was always useful; that they

should continue to watch the man but avoid any public showdown for the time being; we might perhaps find an opportunity to force Lassalle to stand up and be counted, etc., etc.
What do you think of it?[. . .]

Yours, K. M.

Manchester, 7 March 1856

Dear Marx,
[. . .]
Lassalle. It would be a pity about the fellow, because of his great talent, but these things really are too bad. He always was a person to be devilishly closely watched. As a true Jew from the Slav frontier he was always only too ready to exploit anyone for his private purposes under some party pretext. Then this eagerness to thrust himself into elegant society, to climb up, if only for appearance, to plaster over the grimy Breslau Jew with all kinds of pomade and make-up – all this was always repugnant. But then, these were all merely things that called for a sharp lookout. But if he now does things which directly suggest a turn in party line then I cannot blame the Düsseldorf workers for conceiving this hatred of him. I'm going to see Lupus tonight and will put the matter before him. None of us really ever trusted Lassalle but of course one defended him against stupid attacks from H. Bürgers's quarter. It is my view that every-thing should be allowed to run as you have instructed the Düsseldor-fers. If he can be induced to take a direct and manifest step against the party then we've got him. But so far this seems not to have happened and a scandal would anyway be quite out of place.
[. . .]

Yours, F. E.

London, 8 May 1857

Dear Frederick,
Received the £5.
Enclosed a letter from Lassalle which, when you've communi-cated it to Lupus, you'll send back to me early next week. How am I to treat the blighter? Answer or not? The comical vanity of the fellow who wants to become famous at any cost and who, for no

reason at all, writes 75 printer's sheets on Greek philosophy will amuse you.
[. . .]

Yours, K. M.

[. . .]

Manchester, 11 May 1857

Dearest Moor,

Enclosed I'm returning Lassalle's letter. From firtht to latht the thtupid Yid. I can just about imagine the stuff he's scribbled – including the thing that will prove a 'spark' and that he's so mysterious about.

Of course we know that there's nothing to the blighter but it's difficult to find positive grounds for breaking with him, especially as nothing more has been heard from the Düsseldorf workers. He seems – judging by this letter, to have withdrawn from them entirely, or rather they from him, because he has absolutely nothing positive to say on how things are in Germany among the workers. But whether he won't again use a letter from you to boost his standing with them, that's another question. If I were you I would write to him, you can't very well avoid that, but ask him outright how the workers' movement is going on the Rhine, and especially in Düsseldorf, and in that case surely the letter can be so phrased that he'll keep his trap shut about it and that he will either have to declare his position, more or less, or get tired of corresponding with you. Lupus was greatly amused about the letter but our secret council on the matter was interrupted. Incidentally I would also ask him how he came to play your letters into the hands of the police.
[. . .]

Yours, F. E.

London, 22 December 1857

Dear Frederick,

[. . .]

Enclosed a letter (including an enclosure) from the great Lassalle who now positively informs me that he has in fact seriously begun to become well-known in Berlin by his fame. These effusions of a beautiful soul will delight you and Lupus. The good Lassalle managed his philosophy, his Heraclitus, as he did the Hatzfeldt lawsuit and finally, if he is to be believed, won his 'suit'. It does indeed seem that the ancients – philologists and Hegelians – were surprised to experience once more such a *posthumous* flowering of a past era. But we shall see the thing ourselves and, though a gift horse, look deep into its mouth – on the express condition, of course, that this Heraclitus does not reek of garlic. Fancy only this fellow going up and down the streets of Berlin and 'asking for himself' strutting like a peacock, a stride and a stand: biting his lips, with a 'political regard' as who should say: 'This is the man who has written Heraclit'.* Perhaps the fellow might be useful to us in finding booksellers, unless of course he fears that the fame which he is seeking also in the economic field might suffer through competition and his 'suit' might thus be lost.[. . .]

[. . .]

Yours, K. M.

London, 28 January 1858

Dear Frederick,

The great cold that has set in here and the *real coal shortage in our home* compels me – though of all things in the world this is the most distasteful to me – to squeeze you once again. I decided to do so only because of great external pressure. My wife has proved to me that, as a result of a consignment from Jersey which arrived earlier than usual, you have fallen into a calculating error and, unless I specifically wrote to you, would not send anything this month; that she has pawned her shawl, etc., etc., and was at her wits' end. In short, I *must* write and that's why I'm doing it. Indeed if this situation continues I'd rather lie 100 fathoms deep under the earth than continue vegetating like this. Always to trouble others and yet to be perpetually harassed by the most trivial mess is intolerable in the long run. I, personally, work off this *misère* by being very active on general things. My wife, of course, has not the same resources, etc., etc.

Today Lassalle's book arrived, it cost 2 sh., not the price of the

---

* This is Marx's English wording in the original letter (translator's note).

book but the cost of carriage. This circumstance has assured it of a bad reception. 2 volumes of 30 sheets each. Merely glanced into it. In his preface the fellow lies to the public that he'd been pregnant with the thing since 1946. Seems entirely old-Hegelian. In the interpretation and comparison of passages his lawyer's habit of hermeneutics may have helped him. We'll see whether the stuff is too fat to read it through.

[. . .]

Yours, K. M.

London, 1 February 1858

Dear Frederick,

[. . .]

'Heraclitus the Obscure' by Lassalle the Bright is essentially a very silly concoction. With every one of the many images with which Heraclitus develops the unity of affirmation and negation, in walks Lassalle and treats us to some section from Hegel's *Logic* which hardly gains by this process, always at great length – like a schoolboy asked to prove by what he has learnt that he understands his 'essence' and his 'appearance' and the 'dialectical process'. When the schoolboy has mastered that kind of speculation one may be sure that he can nevertheless perform the mental process accurately only in accordance with the prescribed recipe and in the hallowed forms. This is exactly the case with our Lassalle. The blighter seems to have tried to make Hegelian logic clear to himself by means of Heraclitus and to have never tired of resuming that process again and again. As for erudition, there's an enormous exhibition of that. But anyone familiar with this knows how cheap it is – provided one has the time and money and, like Herr Lassalle, gets the Bonn University library sent direct to one's home at one's pleasure – to compile such a display of quotations. You can see how strangely ugly the blighter seems to himself even when arrayed in this philological frippery and how he moves with all the gracefulness of a fellow who is wearing fashionable dress for the first time in his life.[. . .]

[. . .]

But as I wrote to you immediately after his first self-congratulatory letter, the old Hegelians and philologists must

indeed have been pleased to find such old-fashioned substance in a young man who is regarded as a great revolutionary. Besides he flatters and kowtows in all directions in order to make sure of a favourable reception. As soon as I've dipped into the stuff I'll send it to you.
Salut.

Yours, K. M.

London, 18 May 1859

Dear Engels,
[. . .]
Lassalle's pamphlet is an enormous blunder. The appearance of your 'anonymous' pamphlet *Po and Rhine* would not let him rest. Admittedly the position of the revolutionary party in Germany is difficult at this moment, yet it is clear enough after some critical analysis of the circumstances. As for the 'governments', the demand must evidently be addressed to them, from every point of view, if only in the interest of Germany's *existence*, that they should *not* remain *neutral*, but, as you rightly say, be *patriotic*. The revolutionary aspect is to be given to the affair simply by emphasizing the contrast *against Russia* even more strongly than that against Boustrapa.* That's what Lassalle should have done against the anti-French shouting of *Neue Preussische Zeitung. This* is also the point which in effect, in the further course of the war, will drive the German governments into treason against the Reich, and where one will collar them. Incidentally, if Lassalle presumes to speak on behalf of the party he will have to be prepared in future either to be openly disavowed by us, seeing that the circumstances are too important for personal consideration, or, instead of following the mixed inspirations of fire and logic, he must inform himself beforehand of the views of other people beside himself. We must

---

* Nickname for Louis Napoleon Bonaparte, formed from the first syllables of Boulogne, Strasbourg and Paris. The nickname alludes to Bonaparte's attempts to stage Bonapartist coups in Strasbourg on 30 October 1836 and in Boulogne on 6 August 1840, and finally to the Paris coup d'état of 2 December 1851 which led to the establishment of Bonapartist rule in France (editor's note).

now at all costs insist on party discipline, or everything will end up in a mess.
[. . .]

Yours, K. M.

London, 10 June 1859

Dear Frederick,

Today received two manuscripts. *One splendid*, yours on 'Fortification', and indeed I have pangs of conscience for taking up your scant spare time in this way. *One grotesque*, to wit a report by Lassalle to me and you concerning his 'Sickingen'. A whole forest of closely written pages. Incredible how a man at this time of year and under these world-historic circumstances not only finds the leisure to produce that sort of thing but actually expects us to find the time to read it.
[. . .]

Yours, K. M.

London, 9 February 1860

Dear Engels,

[. . .]

By the way, to return to the above-mentioned oaf, i.e. Lassalle. Since I didn't know, when I received his first letter, whether you had already written to him in line with our original arrangement (when circumstances were still different) I said to him in two lines: I had thought his many months' silence had been due to irritation about my last somewhat rude (it was rude as hell) letter. Glad that this was not the case. I had already confided my misgivings to you. Well! The fuss the idiot makes about it! The way the blighter gives himself moral airs *vis-à-vis* Liebknecht! And that's the fellow who uses the most shameless means and has associated with the most shameless persons in the services of the Countess von Hatzfeldt. Has the clot forgotten that, although I wanted to enlist him into the League, it was by unanimous resolution of the central authority in Cologne that he was not accepted because of ill repute? In fact, I believe that out of a sense of delicacy I kept all this from the man, also the workers' deputation which was sent to me from Düsseldorf a few years ago and produces the most scandalous and often irrefutable accusations against him! And now look at that pompous ape! No sooner does he believe – looking through his Bonapartist-tinted spectacles – that he has caught us out in a weak spot – and look how he puffs himself up, how he acts the oracle, how he starts (though prettily) to posture. On the other hand, look how his fear that I might not let myself by pushed aside quite so easily by Vogt, to the benefit of my tender friend Lassalle, makes him lose all his lawyer's instinct! How he contradicts himself! How vile he turns! One should not 'stir up' the business even further. 'One' might not 'take it in good part'. Not take it in good part! One! To please his small-beer philistines I am to allow schoolmaster Squeer, alias Zabel, to dance on my head! I'm quite clear now about Mr Lassalle.

[. . .]

The worst behaviour of all is displayed by that philistine pot-belly Freiligrath. I had sent him the circular. He doesn't even confirm receipt. Does the pig think that, if I felt like it, I could not dunk him in the sulphurous mire to his eyebrows? Has he forgotten that I possess over 100 letters from him? Does he think I cannot see him because he is turning his posterior on me?[. . .]

[. . .]

Yours, K. M.

London, 14 February 1861

Dear Frederick,

I must ask you very much to forgive me for not having replied at once to your very courteous letter. You will meanwhile have received a letter from the philistine Freiligrath.

I had and still have a vast amount of chasing around. The point is I'm intending to go to Holland in order to straighten out my affairs here which would otherwise get too much for me. For that I require two things, passport and money, and I expect I shall find both here one way or another. (Perhaps I'll have to go as far as Aachen.)

I haven't written to Lassalle yet. The business with a weekly would probably be best, but on the other hand think of the risk, given our friend's tactlessness, when he sits right on the spot, in charge of the editorship-in-chief, and is thus in a position to run us all into trouble! He would of course immediately dress up the affair

as a party organ, and thus one would share in the responsibility for any stupidity and ruin one's position in Germany before one has recaptured it. This requires very careful consideration.
[. . .]

Yours, K. M.

London, 7 May 1861

Dear Frederick,
Your accused pleads guilty. But the extenuating circumstances of my failure to write to you are these: first of all you know that I spent the major part of my time in Berlin at Lassalle's house, and there it was *impossible* for me to write to you without telling Lassalle about the letter, and that did not serve my purpose. Later I was continually on the move, from Berlin to Elberfeld, Cologne, Trier, Aachen, Bommel, Rotterdam and Amsterdam. Finally my original plan, as I also wrote to my wife, was to travel from Rotterdam to Hull and from Hull to Manchester, in order to give you an *extensive verbal report* there. This was foiled by my cousin Jacques Philips. Just as I was about to leave Rotterdam he informed me that he would come to London one day later, and he was as good as his word. So of course I had to go straight back to London in order to do the honours there. He only left here the day before yesterday.
[. . .]
First of all then to business. To start with I squeezed 160£ out of my uncle Leon Philips, so that we were able to pay off the major part of our debts. My mother, from whom cash is out of the question, but who is rapidly approaching her break-up, has destroyed a few earlier IOUs I had made out to her. That was a very agreeable result of the two days that I spent with her. I myself did not talk to her of money matters at all, but she took the initiative on that point. Next I cleared the path for myself in Berlin towards making contact, if necessary, with the Vienna *Presse*, which, given the present American circumstances, will probably become indispensable. Finally I arranged, through Lassalle, for the second part of my political economy to be published by Brockhaus instead of by Duncker. As for Duncker, Camilla Essig (alias Ludmilla Assing) observed to me rightly that if you want to keep a book secret you should give it to Duncker to publish.[. . .]
[. . .]

Now for political business.

In Berlin, needless to say, there are no higher politics. Everything turns about the struggle with the police (not as if they were taking the least liberties now; they are a model of courtesy and tolerance), in that one wants to see Zedlitz, Patzke, etc., removed from their offices and punished; secondly about the conflict between military and civilians. These are the issues (in bourgeois circles more specifically the army bills and the tax exemptions for landowners) on which the clash will come. (An artillery officer, Count Tavernier, told me that they would like best to turn their batteries on the Garde du Corps.) There is a general smell of decay about, and people of all ranks regard a catastrophe as inevitable. In the capital things seem to be further advanced in that respect than in the provinces. Strangely enough, even in military circles there is a general conviction that at the *first* collision with the French the Prussians will get hammered. The tone that reigns in Berlin is cheeky and frivolous. The Chambers are despised. I myself have heard a couplet against Vincke sung at a theatre with enormous applause. Among a large part of the public there is great dissatisfaction with the press as it is now. There is now doubt that in the forthcoming new elections (autumn) for the Second Chamber the bulk of the chaps who sat in the Prussian National Assembly will be elected. This is important, not because of those chaps but because 'Wilhelm the Handsome' regards them as red republicans. Altogether our 'handsome Wilhelm' has been haunted by the red spectre ever since he became king. He considers his 'liberal' popularity to be a trap set for him by the revolutionary party.

In these circumstances it would indeed be entirely timely if we could bring out a paper in Berlin next year, repugnant as I personally find the place. 20–30,000 Taler might be scraped together in conjunction with Lassalle. But here is the snag. Lassalle actually proposed this to me. At the same time he confided to me that he would have to be editor-in-chief alongside me. And Engels? I asked him. 'Well, unless 3 is too many Engels might also be editor-in-chief. Except that the two of you could not have more votes than me because otherwise I'd be outvoted every time.' He listed the following reasons why he too would have to be at the head: (1) that he was generally believed to stand closer to the bourgeois party and could therefore more easily raise money; (2) that he would have to sacrifice his 'theoretical studies' and theoretical tranquillity, and surely he would have to have something in return, etc. However, he added, if you don't want this, 'I would be prepared, as in the past, to be of financial and literary assistance to the paper; this would have an advantage for me; I would have the use of the paper without the responsibility', etc.

These of course are sentimental phrases; Lassalle, blinded by the reputation he has in certain scholarly circles thanks to his *Heraclitus*, and in another circles of parasites thanks to his good wine and cuisine, does not of course know that he has a bad name among the broad public. Then there is his know-all attitude; his entrapment in the 'speculative concept' (the fellow is actually dreaming of a new Hegelian philosophy raised to the second power, which he wants to write), his infection with old French liberalism, his prolix pen, his importunity, tactlessness, etc. Lassalle could render good services as one of the editors, under strict discipline. Otherwise he'd expose us to ridicule. But you can see that, in view of the great friendship he displayed to me, I found myself greatly embarrassed about speaking my mind. So I kept to vague generalities, said that I could not decide anything without previous consultation with you and Lupus. (That was the main reason why I did not write to you from Berlin since I did not wish you to reply to Berlin on this point.) If our decision were to be negative the Countess and Lassalle would set out on a journey to the Orient or to Italy for a year. But here's the rub. He now expects an answer from me, and this I can no longer put off. What do you say?

The fellow is frightfully pompous, and I had no other choice than to oppose him with continuous irony which hurt his amour propre, the more so as this aroused in the Countess, whom he had impressed as a universal genius, quite alarming desires for emancipation from this Buddha. Strangely enough the Hatzfeldt woman has, at certain moments, absorbed and memorized from him a Jewish intonation.
[. . .]

Yours, K. M.

London, 11 July 1862

Dear Engels,

Lassalle has been here for 2 days and intends to stay here several weeks. You'll have to come here for a few days because, as it is, he's quite 'offended' that you and Wolff never confirm receipt of his writings. Besides, you wanted to come for a few days to see the exhibition anyway.

I'm writing to you so briefly because I am working like a carthorse on the book.

Salut!

Yours, K. M.

London, 30 July 1862

Dear Engels,

From the enclosed scraps you'll see up to a point how I am bothered. The landlord meanwhile has been pacified, he has to get 25 £. The piano man, who is paid in instalments for the piano, was to have received 6£ on the last day of June, and is a very rude lout. I have tax demands for 6£ in the house. That school muck of about 10£ I have fortunately paid since I'm doing all I can to spare the children direct humiliation. I've paid the butcher 6£ (and this was my total quarterly income from *Presse*!) but the blighter is pestering me again, not to mention the baker, the teagrocer, the greengrocer and whatever the names of those devils are.

That Jewish nigger Lassalle, who is fortunately leaving at the end of this week, has happily again lost 5,000 Taler in a mis-speculation. The blighter would sooner fling his money into the mud than lend it to a 'friend', even if interest as well as capital were guaranteed him. At the same time he proceeds from the view that he has to live as a Jewish baron or baronized (probably by the Countess) Jew. Would you believe it that the blighter, who is aware of the business with America, etc., i.e. is aware of the crisis in which I find myself, had the impertinence to ask me if I wanted to hand one of my daughters over to the Hatzfeldt woman as 'companion' and whether he himself should obtain for me Gerstenberg's (sic) protection! The fellow cost me a lot of time and, so the oaf suggested, since at the moment I had 'no business' but was engaged merely on 'theoretical work', I might just as well kill time with him! In order to observe a certain social propriety *vis-à-vis* the fellow my wife had to take anything that was not actually screwed down to the pawnshop!

If I weren't in this hideous position, and if the parvenu's slapping of his money-bag did not irritate me so, I would have been royally amused. Since I saw him a year ago he has become totally mad. His

81

stay in Zurich (with Rüstow, Herwegh, etc.) and his subsequent journey, and finally his 'Herr Julian Schmidt', etc., have completely gone to his head. He is now by general agreement not only the greatest scholar, the most profound thinker, the most inspired researcher, etc., but also Don Juan and a revolutionary Cardinal Richelieu. And with it that unceasing babbling in his squeaking falsetto voice, his unaesthetically demonstrative movement, his didactic tone!

[. . .]

[. . .] Lassalle was most furious about me and wife for poking fun at his plans, poking fun at him as an 'enlightened Bonapartist', etc. He screamed, raved, jumped about and in the end utterly convinced himself that I am too 'abstract' to understand politics.

[. . .]

As I said, in different circumstances (and if he had not got into the way of my work) the blighter would have royally amused me.

Add to this the immoderate beastlike eating and the randy lust of this 'idealist'.

It is now perfectly clear to me that, as testified also by his cranial formation and hair growth, he is descended from the negroes who joined Moses's exodus from Egypt (unless his paternal mother or grandmother was crossed with a nigger). Well, this combination of Jewish and Germanic stock with the negroid basic substance is bound to yield a strange product. The fellow's importunity is also nigger-like.

[. . .]

Yours, K. M.

[. . .]

London, 2 September 1864

Dear Frederick,

Yesterday afternoon I received the letter from Freiligrath copied below, from which you will see that Lassalle was critically wounded in a duel in Geneva. I went to see Freiligrath the same evening. But he had not received any later telegrams.[. . .]

Yours, K. M.

The death of Lassalle was seen by many of his contemporaries – and by Marx and Engels – as a fitting end for his life, with its mixture of eccentricity, false elegance and qualities reminiscent of Don Quixote: a fleeting affair with Helene von Dönniges led to a duel with her fiancé – with fatal results for Lassalle. From Marx's and Engels's letters it emerges that they were perfectly aware of Lassalle's political significance, despite all the quarrels and intrigues. However, this did not prevent them from commenting, somewhat astonished and mocking at one and the same time, on this operetta-like end, as for example in the striking sentence: 'She didn't want his beautiful mind but his Jewish cock.'

Manchester, 4 September 1864

Dear Moor,

Your telegram arrived yesterday, even before I had opened your letter since all kinds of business immediately took up my time. You may well imagine how the news surprised me. Whatever else Lassalle may have been, as a person, as a literary man, as a scholar – politically he was certainly one of the most significant fellows in Germany. To us at present he was a very uncertain friend, in future a fairly certain enemy, but be that as it may – it does hit one hard to see Germany finishing off all reasonably good people of the extremist party. What jubilation will reign now among the manufacturers and among those progressive pigs. Lassalle after all was the only chap in Germany itself of whom they were afraid.

But what a strange way to lose one's life: to fall seriously in love with the daughter of a Bavarian envoy – that would-be Don Juan – to want to marry her, to clash with a retired rival, who moreover is a Wallachian cheat, and to be shot dead by him. That could only happen to Lassalle, given his strange mixture of frivolity and sentimentality, Jewishness and cavalier posturing that was his and his alone. How could a political man like him shoot it out with a Wallachian adventurer!

[...]

Yours, F. E.

London, 7 September 1864

Dear Frederick,

Lassalle's disaster has been damnably on my mind these days. When all is said and done, he was one of the old stock and the enemy of our enemies. Besides, the thing came as such a surprise that it is hard to believe that such a boisterous, stirring, pushing person is now as dead as a door-nail and has to keep utterly silent. As for the ostensible occasion for his death, you are quite right. It is another of the many tactless actions he committed in his life. With all that I am sorry that during the past few years our relationship was troubled, albeit through his fault.[. . .]

[. . .]

Yours, K. M.

Manchester, 7 November 1864

Dear Moor,

[. . .]

[. . .] Evidently Lassalle's undoing was that he did not immediately fling Helene von Dönniges on to the bed in the guest-house and have a good go at her; she didn't want his beautiful mind but his Jewish cock. It's simply one more affair that could only have happened to Lassalle. That *he* forced the Wallachian to duel is doubly crazy.

[. . .]

Yours, F. E.

Misfortune was a permanent guest at Marx's home. His son Guido, born 1849, died after a year. In 1852 his daughter Franziska also died at the age of one year. No sooner was his daughter Eleanor born in January 1855 than his dearly loved son Edgar, called Musch, died on 6 April. Marx, who had a somewhat blunt attitude to death, was totally crushed; his letters to Engels on the occasion of Musch's death are perhaps the most human testimony of Karl Marx's life. Even in his letter of 8 July 1857, in which he informed Engels of the death of a newly born child, there was still a flash of remembrance of Musch.

London, 3 March 1855.

Dear Frederic!

You'll get a more extensive letter from me on Tuesday. Today just these few lines to explain to you the reasons for my silence:

(1) Musch has a dangerous gastric fever, not yet got rid of (this the worst).

(2) The baby grew every day worse, disturbed the whole house, so that a change of wet nurse necessary a few days ago.

(3) My wife, although childbed passed splendidly, developed a so-called whitlow on the index finger of her right hand. Trivial though this complaint, very intensive and irritating. The thing was operated on yesterday.

(4) Myself first that eye shit, now largely cleared up, then such a loathsome cough that I had to guzzle several bottles of medicine and even keep to my bed for a few days.

You can see the whole house was and largely still is a hospital.

[. . .]

Yours ever, K. M.

[. . .]

London, 16 March 1855

Dear Engels,

I don't believe that dear Musch will overcome his illness. You will understand what effect this prospect is having here at home. My wife is quite low again. At least the matter will soon be decided now.

Yours, K. M.

London, 27 March 1855

Dear Engels,

For the past few days Musch has been visibly improving, and the doctor is voicing the best hopes. If everything goes well Musch must get out into the country at once. He is of course terribly weak and thin. The fever is got rid of, and the abdominal hardening is receding quite markedly. The main question is now merely whether his constitution is strong enough to get through the whole of the treatment. But I believe so. As soon as the physician pronounces the danger to have passed I'll come to you.

[. . .]

Yours ever, K. M.

London, 30 March 1855

Dear Engels,

I've been putting off sending you medical bulletins from one day to the next because the illness has had such ups and downs that my judgement too changed almost every hour. In the end, however, the illness has taken on the character of an abdominal tabefaction, which is hereditary in my family, and hope seems to have been abandoned even by the physician. My wife has for the past week been more sick than ever before, from mental distress. As for me, my heart is bleeding and my head is burning although of course I must keep up a brave appearance. Not for a moment has the child during his illness denied his innate good-tempered and yet independent character.

I cannot thank you enough for the friendship which makes you work in my stead and for the sympathy you are feeling for the child.

Should any turn for the better take place I'll write you at once.

Yours ever, K. M.

[. . .]

London, 6 April 1855

Dear Engels,

Poor Musch is no more. He passed over in his sleep in my arms between 5 and 6 o'clock today. I shall never forget what help your friendship was to us at this terrible time. You will understand my grief for the child. My wife sends you her warmest regards. It is possible that, when I travel to Manchester, I will take her with me for a week, when we would of course put up at a hostelry (or even private lodging). In any case I must find a way of helping her over these first days.

Yours, K. Marx

London, 12 April 1855

Dear Engels,

I intend leaving for Manchester with my wife on Wednesday; she needs a change of scene for a few days. Unless I write to the contrary we'll stick to that date. Anyway I'll write again on Monday.

Our home of course is totally deserted and orphaned since the death of our dear child who had been its life-giving soul. It is indescribable how we miss the child everywhere. I have been through all kinds of bad luck but it is only now that I realize what real misfortune is. I feel broken down. Luckily I have had such a furious headache since the day of the funeral that I am incapable of thinking or hearing or seeing.

Throughout the frightful torments that I passed through these days, the thought of you and your friendship invariably sustained me, as well as the hope that we still have something sensible to do together in this world.

Yours, K. M.

[. . .]

The following letter is an illustration of how even private journeys – Engels's holiday in Ireland in May 1856 with Mary Burns – were governed by aspects of politics and scholarly analysis. In his reflections Engels included the historical observation that the mass destitution in Ireland between 1845 and 1847, caused by the failure of the potato harvest, the principal food crop, had strengthened the Irish national liberation movement during 1847/8. The famine had been transformed into an industrial and trade depression.

Manchester, 23 May 1856

Dear Marx,

On our tour of Ireland we travelled from Dublin to Galway on the west coast, then 20 miles north into the country, then to Limerick, down the Shannon to Tarbert, Tralee, Killarney and back to Dublin. Altogether about 450–500 English miles in the country itself, so that we have seen about two thirds of the whole country. With the exception of Dublin, which is to London as Düsseldorf is to Berlin and entirely bears the character of a former small capital city, and is also built in an entirely English manner, the whole country, and especially the towns, looks as if one were in France or northern Italy, with gendarmes, priests, lawyers, bureaucrats and country estate owners in gratifying numbers and a total absence of any kind of industry, so that it would be difficult to understand what all these parasitical growths were living on if it were not for the hardships of the peasants providing the appropriate companion piece. The 'disciplinary measures' may be seen all over the place, the government is dabbling in everything, not a trace of so-called self-government. Ireland may be regarded as the first English colony, one which, because of its proximity, is still being ruled directly in the old way, and you don't have to go any further than here to realize that the so-called freedom of the English citizen is based on the oppression of the colonies. In no country have I ever seen so many gendarmes, and the type of the Prussian boozy gendarme has reached its highest perfection here in the local constabulary armed with carbine, bayonet and handcuffs.

[. . .]

The country has been totally ruined by the English wars of conquest from 1100 to 1850 (that is how long they went on basically, and also the state of emergency). Most of the ruins testify to destruction during the wars. People themselves as a result have acquired a particular character, and with all the national Irish fanaticism which those fellows have, they feel that they are no longer at home in their own country. Ireland for the Anglo-Saxons! This is now being accomplished. The Irishman knows that he cannot compete with the Englishman who comes here with means superior in every respect; emigration will continue until the predominantly, indeed almost exclusively, Celtic character of the population has gone down the drain. Think how often the Irish have tried to achieve something, and each time they were crushed, politically and industrially. They have artificially, through consistent oppression, become a totally impoverished nation and now, as is well known, it is their job to provide England, America, Australia, etc., with whores, casual labourers, pimps, rascals, cheats, beggars and other criminal rabble. The rabble character clings even to the aristocracy. The landowners, turned bourgeois everywhere else, are here totally turned into rabble. Their country homes are surrounded by enourmous magnificent parks, but all round is waste, and there's nowhere to be seen where the money might come from. Those fellows are the very limit. Of mixed blood, mostly tall, powerful, handsome lads, they all sport enormous moustaches under colossal Roman noses, indulge in the fake military airs of retired colonels, travel about the country in pursuit of all kinds of amusement, and when you make enquiries they don't own a brass farthing, have a pack of debts on their backs and live in fear of the Encumbered Estates Court.

As for the manner in which England governs this country – oppression and corruption, long before Bonaparte tried this – I'll keep that for another time, unless you come here soon. How about it?

Yours, F. E.

Because of Marx's never-ending financial troubles even the death of his former friend and comrade-in-arms Heinrich Heine received no more than a brief mention. Marx had never called Heine's wife Mathilde anything other than 'the bitch' and now pleasurably quoted from Heine's romance The Wife *in order to caricature Mathilde as cheerfully enjoying the poet's death – and in order, in the same breath, to mock Alfred Meissner's recollections, 'inspired' no doubt by Heine himself. Meanwhile the letters of that period reveal that Marx's circumstances, including his family circumstances, were precarious enough.*

London, 1 August 1856

Dear E.,

[. . .]

Received a letter from my wife today. She seems greatly affected by the death of the old lady. She'll have to spend 8–10 days in Trier in order to auction the very insignificant estate of the old lady and to share her proceeds with Edgar. Her plan, as she informs me, is as follows: she will then stay a few more days with a woman friend near Trier. She will then go to Paris and from there straight to *Jersey*, where she has taken it into her head we should spend September and October. Firstly for her own recovery, secondly because it is cheaper and pleasanter than London, and finally because the children would learn to speak French, etc. Naturally she knows nothing of what has happened here. For the moment I am writing to her to say the plan is excellent, even though in fact I cannot see how it can be accomplished.[. . .]

Yours, K. M.

[. . .]

Manchester, 4 August 1856

Dear Marx,
   [. . .]
   I've been waiting from one day to the next for a letter from my old folk summoning me to London. I am arranging things so I can depart on Saturday in case I am summoned. I am moving out on Saturday, I haven't got new accommodation yet nor do I know whether I'll take up any or live as a vagabond for a week, as I intend to do some rather fantastic things upon my return.

My brother-in-law was here, a good fellow, communist from conviction, bourgeois from interest, as he himself states very naively, but always speaks of communist affairs as *We*; tried to persuade me to offer the Prussians a little finger for an amnesty, to which of course I very resolutely replied and eventually he too realized that (1) I couldn't do so and (2) the Prussians would probably tell me to kiss their arse, etc. The man seemed to have few illusions about my state of mind and no doubt left with even fewer – though he was much surprised to find me so merry.
   [. . .]

Yours, F. E.

London, 22 September 1856

Dear Engels,
   [. . .]
   I've received various details about Heine, told to my wife by Reinhardt in Paris. I'll write you at greater length some other time. For now merely that

A few hours after
She was all wine and laughter

was literally true in his case. His corpse was still in the house of bereavement – on the day of the funeral – when the pimp of Mathilde, the angelically gentle, already appeared on the doorstep and in fact took her away. The good 'Meissner', who had spread such soft cowdung around the German public's mouth in connection with Heine, had received cash from that 'Mathilde' in order to glorify this bitch who tortured poor Heine to death.
[. . .]

Yours, K. M.

London, 20 January 1857

Dear Engels,

I am every inch an unlucky fellow. For about 3 weeks Mr Dana has been sending me the daily *Tribune*, evidently just for the purpose of showing me that they are *not* printing *anything* more from me. With the exception of some 40 lines about the manipulations of the Bank of France ('The Crisis in Europe') not a single line of mine has been accepted. From one week to the next I have postponed drawing on *Tribune* because I thought the articles would be printed later, but nothing of the sort. My articles on Prussia, Persia, Austria – all uniformly rejected. Having printed all my things (and also yours) under their own name for about 4 years those pigs have now managed to eclipse my name from the Yankees, just as it was getting known and would have enabled me to find another paper or to threaten them with changing over to another paper. What's to be done? Good advice is at a premium in this situation. The moment I draw they will use the occasion to give me definitive notice, and to write twice a week on the off-chance that among 10 articles one may *perhaps* be printed and paid is too ruinous an arrangement to continue. And how can I draw when nothing is printed?
[. . .]

I am thus totally on the rocks, in accommodation into which I have sunk what little cash I had and where it is impossible to piss my way through from one day to the next as in Dean Street, without prospects and with growing family expenses. I have absolutely no idea what to do and am indeed in a more desperate situation than 5 years ago. I had thought I had swallowed the quintessence of this muck. But no. And the worst of it is that this crisis is not temporary. I don't see how I am to work my way out of it.

[. . .]

Yours, K. M.

[. . .]

Manchester, 22 January 1857

Dear Marx,

Your letter came like a bolt from the blue. I thought everything was at last going well. You in decent accommodation and the business settled; and now it turns out that everything is in jeopardy.[. . .]

[. . .]

During the first few days of February I'll send you £5 and for the time being you can count on this every month. Even if this makes me enter the new accountancy year with a pack of debts, that doesn't matter, I only wish you'd told me about this business a fortnight ago. My old man had made the money for a horse available to me as a Christmas present, and as a good one turned up I bought it last week. Had I known about your business I would have waited a few months and saved the maintenance costs, but never mind, it does not have to be paid straight away. But it does annoy me exceedingly to have to keep a horse here while you and your family in London are in trouble. Incidentally, it is of course understood that this assurance of £5 monthly should not stop you from writing to me additionally in moments of difficulty because I'll do anything that's at all possible. I must altogether embark on a different life, I've gone on far too many sprees lately. Kind regards to your wife and children and let me know soon what you intend to do and how things are.

Yours, F. E.

London, 24 February 1857

Dear Engels,

Are you laughing, are you weeping, are you waking, are you sleeping? Received no answer to several letters sent to Manchester over the past 3 weeks. But I presume that they have arrived. Return to me the enclosure of my last letter – Olmstedt's letter – as I *must* answer it one way or the other.

Yours, K. M.

Manchester, 11 March 1857

Dear Marx,

It's just as if God and the world had conspired to prevent me from writing to you. Just when I think I have surfaced a little from that commercial dizziness I find a whole pile of unsuspected arrears, am overrun by blighters, receive a hundred business enquiries to deal with for my old man, or have to implement some new whims of Mr Gottfried Ermen. To make quite sure I'm tied down Freiligrath saddles me with bill-manipulating Prussian ex-lieutenants who try all day long to borrow money off me (against which he, Freiligrath himself, thought it necessary to warn me) and who after their departure send me pawn tickets so I should redeem their watches with my money! I am not in the least obliged to Freiligrath for that importunate blighter Hugo von Selmnitz he has sent me and have incidentally written to him today about my adventures with that lout, let him mop up the mess himself.

[. . .]

Yours, F. E.

London, 24 March 1857

Dear Engels,

[. . .]

Now to private affairs. First, a letter has arrived from *Tribune* which I'll send you the moment I've answered it. My threat of approaching another paper has evidently had its effect, at least up to a point. In spite of the *very amicable* tone it is evident that I have understood those gentlemen correctly. This is their proposition: *one article* per week they will pay for, whether they print it or not; the *second* I will send at my risk and draw on it *if* they print it. In essence, therefore, they are reducing me to one half. Nevertheless I am *agreeing to it* and *must agree to it*. Even if affairs in England develop

93

the way I think they will I shall yet, after some time, climb back again to my old income.

I am exceedingly sorry that for the time being I still have to pester you since the arrears into which I have fallen have resulted in anything pawnable having already been pawned and the loss of revenue cannot be covered until I have opened up new sources. Besides, since of course I cannot conceal this fact from you, my wife is in an exceedingly interesting condition. However, there was no other purpose at all to my last letter than to explain to you my protracted failure to reply. You will understand that even those with the greatest equanimity – and I do, indeed, possess a lot of equanimity in such a mess – now and again lose their patience and let fly a bit especially *vis-à-vis* friends.

[. . .]

Yours, K. M.

[. . .]

London, 23 April 1857

Dear Fred,

[. . .]

[. . .] Our Freiligrath is again dissatisfied with his post though he very comfortably earns 300 £stg. and has virtually nothing to do. What annoys him is, on the one hand, the grumbling and growling of the shareholders who vent their irritation on him, and partly the admittedly ambiguous position which piles a lot of responsibility upon him without, at the same time, leaving him more than a semblance of independence. So, at least, he himself explains his malaise. What is in fact behind it is, so it seems to me, a general reluctance to take responsibility. A position as a clerk, which relieves him of responsibility, such as the one with Hood, is and remains his ideal. Then he is also troubled by the conflict between his poetic fame and the rate of exchange. As far as I can judge from his occasional confessions, all these *Crédit mobilier* are secretly accompanied by great anxieties. An old London stock exchange stag has assured him that in 40 years' standing he has not come across the kind of chronic crisis that is reigning at present. I have not got round to it yet, but I really must carefully investigate the rela-

tionship between exchange rate and bullion some day. The role which money plays as such in determining the rate of interest and the moneymarkets is something striking and quite antagonistic to all laws of political economy.[. . .]
[. . .]

Yours, K. M.

London, 8 July 1857

Dear Frederic,

My wife has at last given birth. The child, however, was not viable and died at once. In itself no tragedy. But partly circumstances directly connected with it terribly affected my imagination; partly the circumstances which produced this result of such nature that recollection most painful. Impossible to deal with that subject in a letter.

Salut. Give my regards to Lupus and pass the news on to him.

Yours, K. M.

Manchester, 11 July 1857

Dear Marx,

I only received your few lines at the office this morning; the warehouseman who usually brings the mail found it more convenient to do my deliveries in the morning instead of the evening before. The contents of your letter deeply shocked me, in spite of the mystery, because I know things have to be tough for you to write like this. The death of the child is something you can accept stoically, but hardly your wife. You don't say how *she* is, I'm drawing the best conclusion but let me know *positively*, otherwise my mind won't be really at ease. Your mysterious hints leave room to many suppositions in that respect. Provided she is well then ultimately it is for the best that the matter is now over.
[. . .]

Your old F. E.

Manchester, 31 December 1857

Dear Moor,

[. . .]

I went fox-hunting on Saturday, 7 hours in the saddle. Such a thing always excites me hellishly for a few days, it is the most magnificent physical pleasure I know. In the whole field I saw only 2 who rode better than me, but they also had better horses. This is going to put me on my feet again as far as my health goes. At least 20 fellows fell off their horses or crashed, 2 horses were wrecked, 1 fox killed (I was in at the kill); otherwise no mishaps. Incidentally, the genuine fox-hunters were not with us, they of course ride much better than I do. The business for Lupus will be seen to.

[. . .]

Yours, F. E.

Manchester, 11 February 1858

Dear Moor,

[. . .]

Unfortunately I can't send you anything today. I allowed myself to be persuaded to go to a coursing meeting, when hares are chased by hounds, and had 7 hours in the saddle. Although this has generally done me a great deal of good, it prevented me from working.[. . .]

[. . .]

Incidentally, so you should not get any false ideas about my physical condition I will also tell you that yesterday on my mount I jumped over an embankment and hedge 5 foot and a few inches high, the highest jump I've ever made. Such exertions, if they are to be made in comfort, presuppose fairly sound limbs. Altogether we'll give the Prussian cavalry a riding lesson or two when we get back to Germany. Those gentry shall find it difficult to keep up with me, I now have a lot of practice and am improving every day; my reputation is also gradually being established. But I am only now beginning to realize the real problems of riding in difficult terrain, that is a most complicated business.

[. . .]

Yours, F. E.

[. . .]

London, 29 April 1858

Dear Frederick,

I can explain my long silence to you in a single word – inability to write. This existed (and to some degree exists still) not only in the figurative but also in the literal sense of the word. The few unavoidable articles, 'The French Trials in London', 'France's Financial Situation', 'Mr Disraeli's Budget', and 'The British–French Alliance' for *Tribune* I dictated to my wife, but even that was possibly only by applying strong stimuli. I have never before had such a violent attack of my liver trouble, and for some time there were fears of a hardening of the liver. The doctor wanted me to travel but for one thing this was incompatible with the state of finance* and for another I have been hoping from one day to the next I'd be able to get down to work again. The continuing urge to get down to work and then again one's inability to do so helped to worsen the condition. However, things have been better for the past week. Even so I'm not yet capable of work. If I sit down for a few hours and write I then have to lie totally fallow for several days. I am most devilishly anxious for this state of affairs to come to an end next week. It could not have come at a more inconvenient time. Clearly I overdid night work during the winter. Hence those tears.

[. . .]

Yours, K. M.

London, 15 July 1858

Dear Engels,

First of all I would ask you not to be alarmed at the contents of this letter since it is in no way intended as an appeal to your anyway unduly stressed cash-box. On the other hand it is necessary for us to reflect jointly whether some way may be found out of the present situation because this is absolutely no longer tolerable. Its immediate result has already been that I am completely disabled for work because not only do I waste my best time chasing around on useless attempts to raise money but also my power of concentration, perhaps because of my being physically run down, no longer stands up to my pitiful domestic circumstances. My wife is nervously debilitated by this mess, and Dr Allen, who probably suspects where the

---

* This is Marx's original English wording (translator's note).

shoe pinches but of course is unaware of the true state of affairs, has now repeatedly and positively declared that he cannot be responsible for meningitis or something of that kind unless she is sent to a seaside resort for a longish period. As for myself, I know that under the present circumstances the latter, even if it were possible, would not help her so long as she is haunted by the daily pressures and the spectre of an inevitable final catastrophe. This latter, however, cannot be long postponed, and even a remission for a few weeks will not put an end to this intolerable daily struggle about the mere necessaries and will leave the general situation such that everything must come to grief because of it.

Since there are in London alleged loan-societies which advertise loans of 5–200 £ *without securities*, merely with references, I attempted such an operation, with Freiligrath and a grocer offering to act as referees. The result was that about 2 £stg. was spent on fees. The last negative reply arrived the day before yesterday. I don't know if I should make one more attempt of this kind.

[. . .]

[. . .] Even if I were to proceed towards the most extreme reduction of expenditure – e.g. take the children from school, move into purely proletarian accommodation, get rid of the maids, live on potatoes – even then the sale by auction of my furniture would not be sufficient to satisfy even the neighbourhood creditors and ensure an unimpeded departure for some hiding place. The appearance of respectability, maintained until now, was the only means of preventing a collapse. For my part I wouldn't care a damn about living in Whitechapel if only I had an hour's peace again and could cope with my work. But for my wife in her present condition such a metamorphosis could be accompanied by dangerous consequences and for the growing girls it would likewise be scarcely suitable.

I have now made a clean breast of it, and I assure you that it cost me no small effort. But surely I must speak openly to some one at least. I realize that you personally cannot change things. What I ask is merely to have your views on what to do. I would not wish my worst enemy to have to wade through the quagmire in which I've been stuck for 8 weeks, and what's more with furious anger at seeing my intellect wrecked and my working capacity broken by all this unspeakably lousy business.

Yours, K. M.

[. . .]

Although part of the 'economic shit' was now finished – On the Critique of Political Economy – *Engels, usually ready to help in any way, seemed somewhat unenthusiastic about offering to write a few reviews to support the book.*

London, 21 January 1859

Dear Engels,

The unfortunate manuscript is finished but cannot be despatched because I haven't got a penny for posting and registering it. The latter is necessary since I possess no copy of it. I must therefore request you to send me a little money by Monday (post office at Tottenham Court Road corner). If you could send 2 £ that would be most welcome since I have postponed until Monday a few absolutely no longer refusable demands by small people. You will understand that it is by no means pleasant for me to throw myself on you again just now when you have paid, or have to pay, the bill of exchange to Freiligrath. But inflexible necessity. I will see next week – as I'm giving myself a week's holiday with regard to the *continuation* of the manuscript – if I can at all succeed in making some financial coup. I do not believe that 'money' has ever been written about amidst such a shortage of money. Most authors on this subject were utterly at peace with the subject of their researches.

If the business in Berlin comes off it is possible that I shall get out of all this mess.* It is high time.

Salut.

Yours, K. M.

[. . .]

London, 25 May 1859

Dear Fred,

[. . .]

Lupus is greatly mistaken about Liebknecht if he believes that solid citizen could himself accomplish such a rag as *The Reich Regent*. Biskamp wrote the thing (I gave him the facts) and Biskamp

---

* Marx hoped, despite all assertions to the contrary, for some sort of professional break in Berlin, either in publishing or editing a newspaper (editor's note).

has to write *everything*. The only thing from Liebknecht is the 'Political Panorama', London, signed *II*, and not even this in its entirety. Liebknecht is as useless as a writer as he is unreliable and a weak character, a matter on which I shall have to report some details again. The blighter would have received a definite parting kick in his behind this week if certain circumstances were not compelling me to use him as a scarecrow for the time being.

[. . .]

Yours, K. M.

London, 22 July 1859

Dear Engels,

[. . .]

You forgot to write whether you want to do a review of my publication. Jubilation among the blighters here is very great. They think the matter has fallen through *because* they don't know that Duncker has not even advertised it so far. In the event of you writing something the points not to be forgotten are (1) that Proudhonism has been extirpated root and branch (2) that even in its simplest shape, that of the product, the *specifically* social and by no means *absolute* character of bourgeois production has been analysed. Herr Liebknecht has told Biskamp that 'never has a book *disappointed* him so much' and Biskamp himself told me that he could not see any point in it. Is Lupus back?

[. . .]

Yours, K. M.

[. . .]

Manchester, 25 July 1859

Dear Moor,

[. . .]

It is amusing that you have achieved such a pretty verdict also from Herr Liebknecht. Those are the real people. Those gentlemen are so used to us thinking for them that they invariably and everywhere want everything ready cooked and dried, and in convenient small mouthfuls, not just the quintessence but also the detailed exposition. One should work miracles, no more and no less. What does such an ass really want? As if he could not comprehend from

the first 3 lines of the preface that this first issue must be followed by at least 15 others before he gets to the final result. Of course the solutions of the ticklish money questions, etc., are pure muck for Liebknecht since such questions do not even exist for him. But one might at least expect such an oaf to remember at least those points which fit into his own slight concerns. We are just casting pearls before swine.
[. . .]

Yours, F. E.

Manchester, 3 August 1859

Dear Moor,

Enclosed the beginning of the article about your book. Read it carefully, and if you don't like it generally just tear it up and tell me your opinion. I am so out of touch with this kind of writing, through lack of practice, that your wife will laugh a lot about my clumsiness. If you can dress it up do so. A few striking examples of materialist philosophy would be in order instead of that limp one of the February revolution.
[. . .]

Yours, F. E.

London, 27 February 1861

Dear Engels,

I am leaving tomorrow, but with a passport for Holland made out not for me but for Bühring.* It meant an enormous amount of trouble, both this and raising enough money to enable me to leave. Very small on-account payment made to the most urgent creditors; with other (e.g. shopkeepers) referred to American depression and obtained postponement, but only on condition that during my absence my wife would pay *weekly*. In addition she has to pay 2 £ 18 tax next week.

Nota bene. No doubt you've received the letter from my wife (about a week old) thanking you for the wine? She is a little worried that it might have fallen into the wrong hands. The children too very grateful for the wine. They seem to have inherited the paternal liking for drink.

I shall probably also go to Berlin – without passport, to see if the business with a weekly (by the way, Wilhelm I is known in Berlin as *'handsome Wilhelm'*) is possible, and to have a look at the mess generally.
[. . .]

Yours, K. M.

[. . .]

* Bühring formerly represented Faucher's proletariat, his free-trade proletarians – a real inventive genius but not a businessman, hence invariably cheated while others exploited his inventions [Marx's note].

London, 6 November 1861

Dear Frederick,
[. . .]
I had an answer from my old lady yesterday. Nothing but 'tender' phrases, but no cash. Besides she informed me of what I had long known, that she is 75 and feels some of the ills of old age.
[. . .]

Yours, K. M.

Manchester, 28 February 1862

Dear Moor,
I'm despatching a case to you today, carriage paid, containing:

8 bottles Bordeaux
4 bottles old Rhine wine 1846
2 bottles sherry

I have no port that would be suitable. I hope it will do Jenny good. Poor child! Besides I think the thing is of no importance. She has a strong physique, and with nursing and exercise she will no doubt soon regain her strength.

As for the two pounds for the man Koller, I'll be getting them for you tomorrow or Monday.

I am spending more this year than my income. The depression affects us greatly, we have no orders and from next week our workers will be on half time. Yet I must get that £50 for Dronke in four weeks, and pay a year's rent for my rooms in the course of the next week; I'm leaving here; that damned Sarah this morning stole my money from my coat pocket. *Nothing more* therefore to be addressed to Thorncliffe Grove. I'm now living almost entirely at Mary Burns's place in order to spend as little money as possible; unfortunately I cannot manage without lodgings, otherwise I'd move in with her altogether. I haven't got new lodgings yet and must go and look for some. Write again soon how things are. How's the *Tribune*?

[. . .]

Yours, F. E.

London, 19 May 1862

Dear Engels,

A week ago last Thursday you wrote me that you wanted to send me wine for little Jenny and her friends. I showed the children your letter. When the wine did not arrive that was a disappointment. This is important to me at this moment because it cheers them up and things are otherwise very gloomy at home.

[. . .]

Yours, K. M.

Manchester, 30 July 1862

Dear Moor,

I was sorry not to be able to come on Friday, apart from other reasons there was also the fact that I had had something of a quarrel with Ermen and therefore could neither ask a favour from him nor stay away without saying a word. Otherwise I would certainly have come, even at the risk of missing something important on Saturday.

[. . .]

Sincerely yours F. E.

The death of Mary Burns, Friedrich Engels's woman friend, marked one of the low points in the friendship between the two men. He had lived with her and her sister Lizzy in a small house on the edge of Manchester – a liaison which Marx's wife, deeply rooted as she was in bourgeois ideas of matrimony, never approved. She had always maintained a somewhat frosty reserve towards her husband's friend, declined to greet him or his companion if they met anywhere, never called him otherwise than 'Herr Engels' and had never accepted any of his numerous invitations.

Marx himself had evidently regarded the liaison as a lighthearted amusement, a gallant little adventure by his friend, the sort of thing that was accepted with a wink among men. For Engels, however, the relationship had had a totally different significance: it had been his alternative world, whose existence helped him to survive 'that foul commerce'. Fortunately he probably never discovered the mockery with which Jenny Marx, and indeed also his friend, talked about his misalliance, the smugness with which they chuckled at this officially concealed non-legitimated love affair between a working-class girl and a wealthy entrepreneur. Marx's mean-spirited reaction to the news of her death is explained by this attitude.

Manchester, 7 January 1863

Dear Moor,

Mary is dead. Last night she went to bed early, and when Lizzy wanted to lie down to sleep towards 12 o'clock she was dead already. Quite suddenly, heart condition or stroke. I only found out this morning; on Monday evening she was still quite well. I cannot tell you how I feel. The poor girl loved me with her whole heart.

Yours, F. E.

London, 8 January 1863

Dear Engels,

The news of Mary's death has both surprised and shocked me. She was very kindhearted, witty and clung to you firmly.

The devil knows why nothing but bad luck is dogging our circles now. Myself too, I absolutely no longer know whether I'm coming or going. My attempts to raise money in France and Germany have failed, and it was of course predictable that with 15 £ I could hold off the avalanche for a few weeks only. Apart from the fact that we are not getting anything else on credit, except butcher and baker, which also ceases at the end of this week, I'm being pressed for school fees, for the rent and by the entire pack. The few who received a few pounds on account cunningly pocketed the money in order to fall upon me now with redoubled violence. What's more, the children have no clothes or shoes to walk out in. In short, hell is let loose, as I clearly foresaw when I went to Manchester and sent my wife to Paris as a last desperate stroke. Unless I succeed in raising a major sum, through a loan-society or life assurance (and I see no prospect of that; with the first society all my attempts were in vain. They demand surety and insist on production of rent and tax receipts, which I cannot do), we'll hardly manage for another two weeks.

It is hideously selfish of me to be telling you these atrocious things at this moment. But the medicine is homeopathic. One misfortune distracts from another. And, finally and ultimately, what am I to do? There is not a single person in the whole of London to whom I can speak at all freely, and in my own home I act the taciturn stoic to balance the outbursts from the other side. Work under such circumstances becomes utterly impossible. Why not instead of Mary my mother, who anyway is now full of physical ills and has thoroughly lived out her life...? You see what strange ideas the pressure of certain circumstances can produce in 'civilized people'.

Salut.

Yours, K. M.

What arrangements will you make about your establishment now? It is exceedingly tough for you seeing that with Mary you had a home, free and removed from all human muck, whenever you felt like it.

Manchester, 13 January 1863

Dear Marx,

You will think it in order that this time my own misfortune and your frosty reaction to it have made it positively impossible for me to answer you any sooner.

All my friends, including philistine acquaintances, have shown me more sympathy and friendship on this occasion, which inevitably affected me quite closely, than I had a right to expect. You found the moment suitable for a demonstration of the superiority of your cool manner of thinking. So be it!

You know the state of my finances, you know also that I am doing everything to snatch you out of your misfortune. But as for the major sum that you mention, I cannot raise that now as you too must realize. [...]

[...]

Yours, F. E.

London, 24 January 1863

Dear Frederick,

I thought it wise to allow some time to elapse before answering you. Your position on the one hand and mine on the other made it difficult to react to the situation 'coolly'.

It was very wrong of me to write you the letter I did, and I regretted it the moment it was sent off. But it was certainly not done from heartlessness. My wife and children will testify that I was just as shocked when your letter arrived (it came in the early morning) as if one of my nearest and dearest had died. But when I was writing to you in the evening it was done under pressure of very desperate circumstances. I had the broker in the house from my landlord, a protested bill of exchange from the butcher, a shortage of coal and victuals in the house, and little Jenny in bed. Under such circumstances I can generally help myself only by cynicism. What made me especially mad was the circumstance that my wife thought *I* had not informed you of the real state of affairs with sufficient accuracy.

[...]

Yours, K. M.

[...]

Manchester, 26 January 1863

Dear Moor,

Thank you for your honesty. You will yourself realize the impression your last but one letter made on me. One cannot live with a

woman for so many years without being terribly affected by her death. I felt as though I were burying with her the last piece of my youth. When I received your letter she was not yet buried. I can tell you your letter stuck in my mind for a whole week, I could not forget it. Never mind, your last letter makes up for it, and I am glad not to have also lost my oldest and best friend together with Mary.
[. . .]

Yours, F. E.

London, 28 January 1863

Dear Frederick,
[. . .]
I can now tell you without further ado that in spite of the pressures under which I have lived during these past few weeks nothing pressed on me even remotely as much as the fear that there might now be a rift in our friendship. I have repeatedly declared to my wife that I do not care at all about the whole mess compared with the fact that because of these lousy bourgeois troubles and her eccentric excitement I was even capable of assaulting you with my private needs instead of comforting you at such a moment. Consequently domestic peace was greatly upset and the poor woman had to take the whole blame for a thing of which she was in fact innocent to the extent that women are wont to demand the impossible. She had of course no idea what I had written, but with a little reflection she might have worked it out for herself that something of the kind was bound to result. Women are funny creatures, even those equipped with much intelligence. In the morning my wife was crying over Mary and your loss, so that she completely forgot her own misfortune which happened to culminate on that very day, yet by the evening she believed that apart from us there could not be a single soul in the world with any suffering unless he had the broker in the house and had children.
[. . .]

Yours, K. M.

[. . .]

London, 2 December 1863

Dear Frederick,

Two hours ago a telegram arrived that my mother is dead. Fate demands one of the family. Myself, I already had one foot in the grave. In the given circumstances, however, I am clearly more necessary still than the old woman.

I must go to Trier for the settlement of the inheritance. Was very doubtful about what Allen would say as I have only been taking a daily ½ hour's convalescence walk for the past three days.

Allen, however, sending me off with 2 enormous bottles of medicine, actually considers it good for me to go. The wound has not yet stopped festering but I shall find enough Samaritan ladies along the entire journey to apply the plaster.

I must now ask you to send me *immediately* enough money for me to start out on my journey to Trier *at once*.

Salut.

Yours, K. M.

After a great many years and torments Das Kapital *was finished. The most diverse phases of its genesis are attested in numerous letters; in the correspondence with and about Lassalle – who, after all, tried to find a publisher for it – this book also plays the principal part. Nevertheless it left a strangely faint reflection in the correspondence – beginning with the horrendous laconic statement with which Marx in 1859 despatched the preliminary study* On the Critique of Political Economy, *saying that he had no money to post the 'unfortunate manuscript', and using the now-famous sentence 'I do not believe that "money" has ever been written about amidst such a shortage of money', up to the depressing reception of the book in Germany. Liebknecht, for instance, had burst into tears of disappointment. Marx now embarked upon a year-long battle for his book and began by demanding supporting fire from Engels who was made to write a number of reviews – including negative ones – in order to stimulate discussion. There was a perceptible note of reserve in Engels's letter accompanying his first review.*

Nevertheless these years marked a turning point for Marx. Engels's perceptive statement, 'I have always felt that this damned book, over which you gestated for such a long time, was the basic core of all your misfortunes and that you would or could never get out of them until you had shaken it off', betrayed an exact appreciation of the situation, an insight into Marx's dilemma. And the end of the decade eventually saw the 'salvation': Engels succeeded in reaching agreement with 'Monsieur Ermen' the 'pig', the partner in the firm of Ermen & Engels, and he was bought out with a lifelong pension which he would share with Marx.

On 1st July 1869 Engels jubilantly announced to Marx: 'Hurray! Today sweet commerce is at an end, and I a free man.'

Manchester, 2 November 1864

Dear Moor,

[. . .]

Schleswig is a curious country – the east coast very pretty and rich, the west coast also rich, in the middle heathland and waste. The bays all very beautiful. The people are decidedly one of the greatest and most difficult human races on earth, especially the Friesians on the west coast. One only has to travel through the country to convince oneself that the main nucleus of the English come from Schleswig. You know those Dutch Friesians, especially those colossal Friesian women with their fine white and fresh ruddy skins (which also predominate in Schleswig). These are the prototypes of the Northern English, and in particular those colossal women which are to be found here in England too all are of that decidedly Friesian type. I am convinced that the 'Jutes' (Anglo-Saxon: Eotena cyn) who immigrated to England with the Angles and Saxons were Friesians, and that the Danish immigration into Jutland as into Schleswig does not predate the 7th or 8th century. The present Jutlandic dialect itself is proof of this.

These fellows are great fanatics and that is why I like them a lot. You're sure to have read some things by that strange 'Dr K. J. Clement from Northern Friesia'. That fellow is typical of the whole race. The struggle against the Danes for these fellows is dead serious and their entire life's mission, and the Schleswig-Holstein theory to them is not an end but a means. They regard themselves as a race superior to the Danes both physically and morally and indeed are so. To believe he could handle that kind of people in his way – that really was a fine illusion of Bismarck's. We have held out against the Danes for fifteen years and maintained our territory, and we are now to knuckle under to those Prussian bureaucrats? That's how those fellows talked.

The linguistic and nationality conditions are most particular. In Flensburg, where according to Danish claims the whole northern part is Danish, especially along the port, all the children, who were playing by the port in large numbers, talked *Low German*. North of Flensburg, on the other hand, Danish – i.e. the Low Danish dialect, of which I understand scarcely a word – is the popular language. In Sundewitt the peasants in the tavern, on the other hand, spoke variously Danish, Low German and High German, and neither there nor in Sonderburg, where I always addressed the people in Danish, was I answered in anything but German. At any rate north Schleswig is greatly corroded by Germanization and it would be extremely difficult to make it entirely Danish again, certainly more difficult than German. I would prefer it to be more Danish, because in the end one will have to cede something here to the Scandinavians, for decency's sake.

I have lately concerned myself a little with Friesian–Anglian–Jutlandic–Scandinavian philology and archaeology and I have come to the conclusion, here too, that the Danes are a pure nation of advocates who will *directly and knowingly lie* for party interest even in scholarly questions.[. . .]

The Prussians in Schleswig looked very good, to my astonishment, especially the Westphalians, who looked like giants by the side of the Austrians, though of course also much plumper. The entire army ran about unshaven, also unbuttoned-up and altogether in a most unmilitary manner, so that the dapper Austrians here almost play the part of the Prussians. Among the Prussian artillery and engineering officers I've found some very pleasant fellows who told me all manner of entertaining things: but the infantry and cavalry were most genteelly reticent and also enjoyed a very bad reputation among the populace.[. . .]

[. . .]

Yours, F. E.

London, 4 November 1864

Dear Frederick,

[. . .]

(3) *Bakunin* sends his regards. He left for Italy today, where (Florence) he lives. I saw him yesterday, the first time in 16 years. I must say that I liked him very much, and better than before. With reference to the Polish movement he says this: The Russian government made use of the movement in order to keep Russia itself quiet, but certainly did not expect an 18 months' struggle. They therefore provoked the business in Poland. Poland, he says, went wrong for two reasons, the influence of Bonaparte and, secondly, the hesitation of the Polish aristocracy to proclaim a *peasant socialism* openly, and unambiguously from the start. He (Bakunin) would now – following the collapse of the Polish business – participate only in the socialist movement.

On the whole he is one of the few people who I find after 16 years has developed not backwards but forwards. I also discussed with him Urquhart's denunciations. (Incidentally: the International Association will probably get me at loggerheads with these friends!) He asked a lot about you and Lupus. When I informed him of the latter's death he immediately said the movement had lost an irreplaceable man.

[. . .]

Yours, K. M.

London, 31 July 1865

Dear Engels,

My prolonged silence, as you may have suspected, was due not to the pleasantest of causes.

For the past two months I have practically lived at the pawnshop and hence with accumulated and daily more intolerable pressing demands on me. This fact cannot surprise you if you consider: (1) that throughout the whole period I was unable to earn a farthing, (2) that the mere paying off of the *debts* and the furnishing of the house cost me about 500 £. I have kept account of it (as to this item) penny by penny because I myself found it phenomenal the way the money vanished. Added to this was the fact that all kinds of antediluvian demands were made from Germany, where God knows what stories had been put about.

At first I wanted to come and see you to discuss the matter with you in person. But at this moment any loss of time is irreplaceable to me since I cannot very well interrupt my work. Last Saturday I explained my departure to the sub-committee of the 'International' in order to have at least a fortnight entirely free and undisturbed to get on with my work.

I assure you I would rather have had my thumb chopped off than write this letter to you. It is truly shattering to remain dependent half one's life. The only thought that sustains me is that the two of us are engaged in a partnership business, with me giving my time to the theoretical and party part of the business. True, I live too expensively for my circumstances and, besides, we have lived better this year than usually. But this is the only way in which the children, quite apart from the many things they have suffered and for which they were compensated at least for a short while, can make contacts and connections which might secure their future for them. I believe you yourself will take the view that, even from a purely business point of view, a purely proletarian set-up would have been unsuitable here, although that might serve quite well if my wife and I were on our own or if the girls were boys.

As for my work on *Das Kapital*, I will give it to you straight from the shoulder. Another 3 chapters remain to be written before the theoretical part (the first 3 books) is complete. Then the 4th book, the historical-literary one, remains to be written, which is the relatively easiest part for me since all questions have been solved in the first 3 books and the final one therefore is something like a recapitulation in historical form. However, I cannot make up my mind to send off anything before I have the whole thing before me. Whatever shortcomings they may have, the virtue of my writing is that they are an artistic entity, and that can be achieved only by my method of never having them printed until I have them before me in their *entirety*. This is impossible by the Jacob Grimm method which is altogether more suitable for writings which are not dialectically structured.

[. . .]

Yours, K. M.

Manchester, 7 August 1865

Dear Moor,

[...]

I am very glad to know the book is making rapid progress; from a few turns of speech in your last letter I had really begun to suspect that you had once again arrived at an unexpected turning point that might delay everything to an uncertain date. The day the manuscript is sent off I shall get mercilessly drunk, unless of course you come here the following day and we can do it together.

[...]

Our dear Liebknecht simply cannot keep off tactlessness and indolent scribbling. One will always have to be annoyed with him for 10 months out of 12, the moment he is on his own and has to act off his own bat. But what do you expect? It is simply his Liebknecht nature and no amount of annoyance and no amount of grumbling will change that. And ultimately he is, at the present moment, the only reliable contact we have in Germany.

[...]

Yours, F. E.

London, 10 February 1866

Dear Fritz,

This time it was a close shave. My family did not know how serious the business was. If the thing recurs three or four more times in the same form I am a dead man. I am wonderfully slimmed down and still damned weak, not in my head but in my loins and legs. The doctors are quite right, *excessive night work*, is the main cause of this relapse. But I cannot inform those gentlemen of the reasons – besides, this would be quite pointless – which force me into such extravagant behaviour. At this moment I still have some small after-growths on my body, which are painful but no longer dangerous in any way.

The most repugnant part for me was the interruption of my work which, since 1 January, when my liver trouble disappeared, had been making splendid progress. '*Sitting*' of course was out of the question. That is still uncomfortable at this moment. But I nevertheless kept beavering away even lying down, though only for short periods during the day. I have not been able to make any progress with the really theoretical part. For that my brain has been too weak. [. . .]

[. . .]

Yours, Moor

Manchester, 10 February 1866

Dear Moor,

I have just spoken to Gumpert here and discussed your condition with him. He is definitely of the opinion that you should try arsenic. He has applied it in one case of carbuncles and in one of very violent furunculosis and achieved a complete cure in about 3 months. He is now giving it to 3 women, and so far with excellent result: they are also putting on weight and fat. Fowler's solution is what he prescribes, I think 3 times daily 3 drops (I don't remember it accurately now), but altogether it comes to *about 1 grain of arsenic* daily per patient. Given the specific effect of arsenic on all skin diseases there exists every prospect of a cure here too. Iron, he thinks, would only have a symptomatic and strengthening effect. What's more, no special diet has to be observed with arsenic, *just good living.*

You really must do something sensible to get clear of this carbuncle business, even if it means that the book is delayed by another 3 months. The thing is really getting too serious, and if your brain, as you yourself are saying, is not in top form for the theoretical things, then why don't you rest it a little from higher theory. Leave off night work for some time and lead a somewhat more regular life. When you are all right again come here for a fortnight or so, to have a change of scenery, and bring along a sufficient number of notebooks so that, if you like, you can do a little work here. Besides, those 60 sheets amount to 2 fat volumes. Can't you arrange things so that at least the first volume is sent off to the printer in advance and the second a few months later? In that way both publisher and public would be satisfied and no real time lost.

[. . .]

Yours, F. E.

[. . .]

London, 13 February 1866

Dear Fred,

[. . .]

Yesterday I was lying fallow again because a vicious brute of a carbuncle has erupted on my left thigh. If I had more money, that means more > -0, for my family, and if my book were finished, I wouldn't care in the least whether I am flung into the knacker's yard today or tomorrow, in other words croaked. But in view of the circumstances mentioned this is not yet possible.

As for this 'damned' book, this is how things are: it was *finished* at the end of December. The discussion of ground rent alone, the penultimate chapter, very nearly, in the present version, makes a book of its own. I went to the Museum in the daytime and wrote at night. The new agricultural chemistry in Germany, especially Liebig and Schönbein, who are more important in this matter than all economists taken together, and on the other hand the enormous material which the French have produced since I last concerned myself with this issue, had to be mugged up. I concluded my theoretical studies of ground rent 2 years ago. And in the time since a great deal, incidentally fully confirming my theory, had been achieved. The opening up of Japan (normally as a rule, unless compelled professionally, I never read travel accounts) was also important here. Hence the 'shifting system', just as the English manufacturer beasts applied it to *the same persons* from 1848–50, applied to me by myself.

Although completed, the manuscript, enormous in its present form, is not suitable for delivery to anyone except myself, not even to you.

[. . .]

Yours, K. M.

[. . .]

London, 20 February 1866

Dear Fred,

You can imagine how welcome the £10 was. I had two threats of distraint in the house, for that swinish municipal tax of 6£ 9d. and for the Queen's taxes of 1s. 16d. and the final date was Friday.

As for the carbuncles, this is how things stand:

About the *upper* one I had told you, what with my long experience, that it should really be *lanced*. Today (Tuesday), following receipt of your letter, I picked up a sharp razor, a memento from our dear Lupus, and *cut the swine with my own hand*. (I cannot bear doctors among my genitals or near them. Besides, Allen gives me the testimonial that I am one of the best subjects to be operated upon. I always acknowledge *the necessary*.) The rotten blood, as Mrs Lormier says, flowed, or rather squirted up high, and I now regard this carbuncle as buried even though it still wants some nursing.

As for the *lower* swine, that is getting malign and is *beyond* my control and has kept me awake all night. If this mess continues I shall, of course, have to call Allen since I am unable, because of the location of the swine, to watch and cure it myself. Incidentally it is obvious that, on the whole, I know more about carbuncles than most doctors.

Incidentally, what I *hinted* to Gumpert on my last stay in Manchester continues to be my belief: to wit that the itching and scratching between my testicles and my posterior over the past $2\frac{1}{2}$ years and the *peeling of the skin* as a result, is running me down physically more than anything else. The business started 6 months before the first monster carbuncle which I had on my back, and continues *to this day*.

Dear boy, under these circumstances one is more than ever sensible of the happiness from the kind of friendship that exists between us. You know for your part that *no* relationship is as important to me as this one.

[. . .]

Yours, K. M.

Manchester, 22 February 1866

Dear Moor,

Thanks for *Klein Zaches*,* etc., which I take as proof that you've received the £10.

I've just come from Gumpert, whom I only met tonight because of my influenza and missing him several times. It is his view that you

---

* Short story by E. T. A. Hoffmann (translator's note).

should *start on the arsenic at once.* Under no circumstances can it do you any harm, he says, it can only help. If Allen says it isn't suitable for you then that's nonsense. Next he also regards the treatment with poultices as nonsense; this, he says, merely promotes the *inflammation of the skin*, which on the contrary should be suppressed, while not promoting festering. Ice packs would be much better, but so long as you are in Allen's hands these could of course be applied only if he prescribes them. But above all sea air, so you recover your strength again. Admittedly, a place on the south coast would be preferable because they have more fine weather there than we have here at this time of year, but if you would rather be near Gumpert there are, he says, enough resorts on the coast up here within an hour's ride from Manchester.

As you can see, I have succeeded in getting Gumpert to change his mind so that he now urges you to take arsenic at once, even while Allen is still treating you externally; previously he would not hear of this for reasons of etiquette. But do me the favour now and eat that arsenic, and come up here as soon as your condition makes this at all possible, so that you get really better at last. You're only ruining yourself with this eternal hesitation and procrastination, no one can in the long run bear this chronic carbuncle business, quite apart from the fact that one day one may appear that will assume such proportions that you'll go to the dogs. And where would your book and family be then?

You know that I'm ready to do whatever is possible, and in this extreme situation even more than I could risk in other circumstances. But you be sensible also and do me and your family this one favour of *letting yourself be cured*. What's to become of the entire movement if anything happens to you, and the way you go about things it's *bound* to happen. Truly, I shall have no quiet moment day or night until I know you're clear of this business, and each day I have no news of you I am anxious and think you may be worse again.

Nota bene. On no account should you let it happen again that a carbuncle is not cut when it really should be cut. That I am told is highly dangerous.

Many regards to the ladies.

Yours F. E.

Margate, 6 April 1866

Dear Fred,

[. . .]

I am bound to tell you openly that things are very bad with the 'International', the more so as the congress has been fixed for the *end of May* because of the impatience of the French.

The fact is this, that the English leaders in London, now that we've created a position for them (added to which is every Englishman's inability to do two things at once), are *exceedingly cool* in our narrower movement. My absence throughout nearly 3 months has been *extraordinarily damaging.* WHAT'S TO BE DONE? In France, Belgium, Switzerland (and even here and there in Germany, and indeed sporadically in America) the Association has made great and steady progress. In England the reformist movement, brought into existence by ourselves, nearly killed us. The matter would be of no importance if the Geneva Congress had not been fixed for the end of May, and if the Parisians, for whom this movement is *the only one possible*, had not made it virtually impossible through a special journal, *Le Congrès*, to postpone the congress. The English would soon realize the lousiness of the reformist movement such as it is now. After my return a threat of flirtation with the Potter clique, etc., would soon get everything back in line again. But there is no time. For the English even the failure of the congress is a matter of indifference. But for us? *A European disgrace!* I really see no way out. The English have neglected everything that would have made the congress possible in any decent shape. What's to be done! Do you think I *should travel to Paris* to make the people there see how *impossible* the congress is at this moment? Answer me soon. Only in agreement with the Parisians can I see a possible way out. [. . .]

Yours, K. M.

Manchester, 1 May 1866

Dear Moor,

I hope you've happily got rid of your rheumatism and facial pains and are once more working hard at your *book*. How's it going, and when will the first volume be ready? Besides, you must go on taking the arsenic, it should be taken for at least 3 months and is in no way connected with rheumatism, etc. The liver troubles may have con-

tributed to the carbuncles by upsetting the digestion, or blood formation, and just for that reason you must continue to get a few hours' exercise regularly every day and leave off night work, so that everything is cleared up again. Once a proneness to hyperaemia of the liver is so classically and systematically established as in you it does not of course go away again all of a sudden.
[...]

Yours, F. E.

London, 7 August 1866

Dear Fred,

You correctly observed from my last letter that the state of my health has improved although it fluctuates up and down from one day to another. However, the feeling that one is capable of work again does much for a man. Unfortunately I am continuously interrupted by social troubles and lose a lot of time. Thus e.g. the butcher has suspended meat supplies today, and even my stock of paper will have run out by Saturday.

Since yesterday Laura is half promised to Monsieur Lafargue, my medical Creole. She treated him like the rest, but the emotional extravagance of such Creoles – some fear that the young man (he is 25) might kill himself, etc. – some affection for him, though cold as always with Laura (he is a handsome, intelligent, energetic and gymnastically developed lad) have more or less resulted in a half-compromise. The boy at first clung to me but soon transferred his affection from the old man to his daughter. His economic circumstances are of a middling nature as he is the only child of a former planter's family. He has been relegated from the University of Paris for two years because of the Congrès à Liège, but wants to take his examination at Strasbourg. In my judgement he has an exceptional talent for medicine, although he is infinitely more sceptical in that field than our friend Gumpert. Medical scepticism seems to be the order of the day in Paris among professors and students, e.g. Magendie, who declares all therapeutics to be charlatanism at the present stage. This scepticism, as always, does not exclude crankish views but includes them. Lafargue, for instance, believes in alcohol and electricity as principal therapeutic means.[...]
[...]

Yours, K. M.

London, 13 August 1866

Dear Fred,

[. . .]

You must excuse me if I *don't* write you a letter today. I have the most urgent matters on my plate. I have today written a long letter to Lafargue, in French, notifying him that I must have certain information from his family on his economic circumstances before the affair can progress or develop into an arrangement. A letter which he showed me yesterday from a famous French physician in Paris speaks for him.

[. . .]

Yours, K. M.

[. . .]

London, 23 August 1866

Dear Fred,

Today just a few lines. The affair with Lafargue is arranged to the point that his old man has written to me from Bordeaux, requesting the title of fiancé for his son, offering very favourable economic terms. Moreover understood that Lafargue junior must first take his doctor's examination in London and then in Paris before thinking of marriage. So far the thing is settled. But I also informed our Creole yesterday that, unless he can cool down to English manners, Laura might well show him the door. This he must fully realize, or else the business will come to nothing. He is a thoroughly good chap but spoilt and too much a child of nature.

Laura declares that before getting formally engaged she must have your consent.

[. . .]

Yours, K. M.

London, 19 January 1867

Dear Engels,

After a long silence, for which excessive work was his excuse, Meissner has written to me to say my plan 'did not suit him'.

(1) He wants to have the 2 volumes complete in his hands at the same time; (2) not print in stages, since he wants to deliver one

printer's sheet per day and leave only the final corrections (revision) to me.

I answered him that (2) was a matter of indifference to me since he would shortly be able to have the entire manuscript of Volume I. If he started printing later and printed more quickly it would come to the same thing. But he should consider carefully whether in a book with so many glosses in different languages the kind of correction he wanted was feasible without great disfigurement through printing errors. As for (1) this would be impossible without great delay to the whole business, also by no means so arranged in our contract. I explained to him the various reasons but have not had any answer yet.

Apart from the delay I cannot agree about the 2nd volume, the less so as I must have a break for the sake of my health when the first volume is published and altogether must go to the continent to see if I can regulate my affairs in any way. These are getting worse every day, and everything threatens to collapse about my ears. The baker alone has a demand of 20 £ and all those devils of butcher, grocer, taxes, etc. [. . .]

[. . .]

Yours, K. M.

Manchester, 13 March 1867

Dear Moor,

I did not write to you partly because of all kinds of obstacles but partly also half intentionally because I wanted to let the date pass by which 'The Book' was to be completed, and now hope that it is completed. So when will you go and see Herr Meissner? When you do I shall also give you an assignment so you can collect the fee for my last brochure.

[. . .]

London, 2 April 1867

Dear Engels,

I had determined not to write to you until I could inform you of the completion of the book, which is now the case. I also did not wish to bore you with the reasons for the renewed delay, to wit carbuncles on my behind and in the vicinity of my penis. Their last remains are now fading but they only permitted a sitting position (that is a writing position) at the cost of considerable pain. I am *not* taking arsenic because it makes me too stupid and I had to keep a clear head at least for the time when writing was possible.

I must take the manuscript to Hamburg myself next week. I did not like the tone of Herr Meissner's last letter. Moreover, yesterday I received the enclosed scrap of paper from Borkheim. I have every reason to think that the 'continental friend' is Herr Geheimrat Bucher. The fact is that Borkheim had written a letter to him, which he read to me, in connection with his travelling arrangements to Silesia, where he has to go on family business. Bucher answered him immediately. I therefore suspect an intrigue behind these fairy-tales and must place my knife personally at Meissner's throat. Otherwise I would not put it past the blighter to hold back my manuscript (approximately a good 25 printer's sheets, according to my calculation) and at the same time *not* to have it *printed* on the pretext of wishing to 'await' the second volume.

I must now first of all redeem my clothes and watch, which live at the pawnshop. I can also hardly leave my family in the present situation when they are *sans sou* and the creditors are growing more impudent every day. Finally, lest I forget, all the money that I could spend on Laura's champagne treatment has gone the way of all flesh. She must now have red wine, and better wine that I can command. That's how things are.

[. . .]

Yours, K. M.

Manchester, 4 April 1867

Dear Moor,

Hurray! This exclamation was irrepressible when at last I read in black and white that Volume I is finished and that you want to take it to Hamburg straight away. So that the vital nerve should not be lacking I'm sending you encl. seven half five-pound notes, altogether £35, and shall post the other halves immediately upon receipt of the usual telegram.[. . .]

[. . .]

Yours, F. E.

Hamburg, 13 April 1867

Dear Fred,

I arrived here towards 12 noon yesterday. The ship left London on Wednesday, at 8 o'clock in the morning. You will gather from this the whole story of the voyage. Exceedingly wild weather and gale. Yet I, after being cooped up so long, was feeling like five hundred hogs, so cannibalic jolly.* But the business would have become boring in the long run, what with all the sick and decamping pack right and left if a certain nucleus had not stood firm. This was a very 'mixed' nucleus, to wit a German ship's captain, very similar to you in his features, but a short fellow (he also had a good deal of your humour and the same benignly frivolous twinkle in his eye); a London cattle-dealer, a real John Bull, bovine in every respect; a German watch-maker from London, a pleasant fellow; a German from Texas; and the principal character, a German who has been knocking about in eastern Peru for the past 15 years, a region only recently geographically recorded, where, among other things, human meat is still widely consumed. A fantastic, vigorous and cheerful fellow. He had a very valuable collection with him, of stone axes, etc., worthy of having been found in 'caves'. As an appendix a female person (the other ladies all seasick and vomiting in the ladies' cabin), an ancient mare with a toothless mouth, speaking with a genteel Hanover accent, daughter of an ancient-lineage Hanoverian Minister, von Baer or some such name, now for a long time a trainer of humans, Pietist, improving the situation of the workers, acquainted with Jules Simon, with a very beautiful soul with which she bored our bullish friend to death. Well! Thursday evening, with the gale at its worst, so that all the tables and chairs were dancing, we drank in a small circle, while the elderly female, the mare, was lying on a couch, whence the ship's movement would from time to time – to distract her a little – tip her onto the floor in the middle of the cabin. What kept this beauty captivated under these aggravating circumstances? Why did she not retreat to the women's quarters? Our German savage was recounting with real gusto all kinds of sexual filth practised by the savages. That was the attraction for that delicate, pure, fine lady.† One example: he is a

---

* This is a line from a drinking song in Goethe's *Faust*, I, translation by Baynard Taylor, 1880 (translator's note).

† The phrase is a quotation from a Heine poem (translator's note).

guest in an Indian hut, where the wife is giving birth that same day. The afterbirth is roasted and – supreme gesture of hospitality – he is made to enjoy with them a morsel of this sweetbread!

Immediately upon our arrival I went to see Meissner. Clerk told me he wouldn't be back before 3 o'clock (in the afternoon). I left my card and invited Herr Meissner to dinner with me. He came but had another person with him and wanted me to come along with him as his wife was expecting him. I declined but we agreed that he would visit me at 7 o'clock in the evening. He told me *en passant* that Strohn was probably still in Hamburg. I therefore went to Strohn's brother. Our man had left for Paris that very morning. In the evening, therefore, Meissner arrived. Pleasant fellow, in spite of his slight Saxon intonation, as suggested by his name. After short negotiation everything all right. Manuscript taken immediately to his publishing house, there placed in the safe. Printing will start in a few days and progress rapidly. We drank together then, and he declared his great 'enchantment' at having made my honoured acquaintance. He now wants the book to appear *in 3 volumes*. The point is he opposes the idea of me concentrating the final book (*the historical-literary part*) the way I had intended. He says that from the bookseller's point of view for the 'broad' mass of readers he was placing his highest expectations in just that part. I told him I would be at his disposal in this respect.

At all events, *we* have in Meissner a man entirely at our disposal; he has a great contempt for the entire pack of shoddy litterateurs. As for your little bill, I thought it wise not to present it yet. Always keep the pleasant surprises for last.

And now Adio, old boy.

Yours, K. Marx

Best compliments to Mrs Burns!

On 24 April 1867 Marx wrote to Engels from Hanover: 'Yesterday Bismarck sent me one of his satraps, the lawyer Warnebold (this is between you and me). He wanted me and "my great talents to be utilized in the interests of the German people."' So Bismarck, who had also carried on long conversations and negotiations with Lassalle – to Marx's extreme indignation, who considered this a betrayal – had tried to get in touch with Marx as well during the latter's stay in Germany.

Manchester, 27 April 1867

Dear Moor,

[. . .] I have always felt that this damned book, over which you have gestated such a long time, was the basic core of all your misfortunes and that you would and could never get out of them until you had shaken it off. This eternally unfinished thing weighed you down physically, mentally and financially, and I can very well understand that, having shaken off this nightmare, you now feel an entirely different person, especially as the world, once you enter it again, no longer looks as gloomy as before. [. . .] I am enormously pleased about this whole turn the matter has taken, first for its own sake, secondly for you especially and your wife, and thirdly because it really is about time that all this should improve. In 2 years my contract with the Gottfried pig expires and, the way things are shaping here, it is hardly likely that either of us will wish to extend it; indeed it is not impossible that a separation may occur even sooner. If that is the case I shall have to *get out completely* from commerce, because to start a business of my own now would mean 5–6 years' terribly hard work without appreciable results and then another 5–6 years' hard work in order to glean the fruits of the first 5 years. But that would finish me. There's nothing I long for more than release from this filthy commerce which is totally demoralizing me with its waste of time. So long as I am in it I'm incapable of anything, and since I've been Principal things have become much worse because of the greater responsibility. If it were not for the higher income I would truly prefer to be a clerk again. At any rate, my life as a businessman will come to an end in a few years, and then the income, too, will flow very, very much more sparingly, and that's what I've always racked my brains about, how we shall then arrange matters with you. However, if things continue as they are now beginning then we'll find a way of arranging that too, even if the Revolution does not intervene to put an end to all financial projects. But if that does not come about I reserve the right to treat myself to a huge frolic on my release and to write an entertaining book: *Woes and Joys of the English Bourgeoisie.*

[. . .]

That Bismarck would knock at your door is something I expected, though not in such a hurry. It is significant for the thinking and the horizon of that fellow that he judges everybody by himself. Well may the bourgeoisie admire the great men of today: it sees itself reflected in them. All the qualities which enabled Bonaparte and Bismarck to achieve successes are mercantile qualities: the pursuit of a definite objective through waiting and experimenting until the right moment has been found, the diplomacy of the ever-open back door, compromise and arrangements, the swallowing of insults when one's interest demands it, the 'we don't wish to be thieves', in short the merchant in all things. Gottfried Ermen in his way is as great a statesman as Bismarck, and if one follows the manipulations of these great men one feels transported time and again to the Manchester Exchange. Bismarck thinks: if only I keep knocking at Marx's door I shall eventually find the right amount, and we'll then do a little business together. Gottfried Ermen to a T.

[. . .]

Yours, F. E.

Hanover, 7 May 1867

Dear Fred,

[. . .]

I hope and confidently believe that within a year I shall have established myself to a point where I can fundamentally reform my economic circumstances and at last stand on my own two feet again. Without you I could have never completed the job, and I assure you that it has always weighed on my conscience, like a nightmare, that you were wasting your splendid strength on commerce and allowing it to rust chiefly for my sake and, into the bargain, had to share in all my petty troubles. I cannot, on the other hand, conceal from myself the fact that I still have a year of trials before me. I have taken a step on which a lot depends, on which, to be precise, it will depend whether a few 100£ will be placed at my disposal from the only quarter from which this is possible. There is a tolerable prospect of a positive outcome though I shall be kept in suspense for about 6 weeks. I shan't have a definite decision before then. What I fear most – apart from the uncertainty – is my return to London, which will nevertheless become necessary in 6–8 days. My debts there are considerable, and the tiresome debtors are 'urgently' waiting for me to return. Then once more the family troubles, the internal clashes, the mad chase instead of getting down to work briskly and unharassed.

[. . .]

Yours, Moor

Manchester, 16 June 1867

Dear Moor,

I have been so disturbed for the past week by all kinds of rowing with Monsieur Gottfried and other such affairs and interruptions that I have only had rare moments of quiet for the study of the value aspect. Otherwise I would have long returned the sheets to you. Sheet 2 in particular has a somewhat depressed carbunculous appearance, but that cannot now be changed, and I don't think you should do any more about it in the Appendix since the philistines are not accustomed to this kind of abstract thought anyway and will certainly not torment themselves for the sake of the value aspect. At the most one might adduce somewhat more extensive historical support for what has been dialectically derived, subjecting it, as it were, to the test of history, although in fact the most necessary points have already been made. But you have so much material on the subject that surely you could make a perfectly good digression about it, one that would prove to the philistines, by the historical method, the necessity of money formation and the process that accompanies it.

You made a big mistake in not making the logical steps of these more abstract arguments more readily accessible by a greater number of small sub-divisions and sub-headings. You should have treated this part in the manner of Hegel's encyclopaedia, with short paragraphs, each dialectical transition emphasized by a separate heading and all digressions and mere illustrations set, if possible, in a special type. The thing might have looked a little didactic but it would have made comprehension considerably easier for a very large class of readers. After all, the *populus*, even the learned, is no longer used to this kind of thinking, and one should therefore give them all possible help.

By comparison with the earlier presentation* there is very marked progress in the acuteness of the dialectical argument, though as for the presentation itself I like certain things better in their first shape. It is a great pity that the important second sheet suffers from this carbuncle pressure. But nothing can be done about that now, and anyone capable of dialectical thought will surely understand it.[. . .]

Yours, F. E.

[. . .]

London, 16 August 1867

Dear Fred,

Just finished correcting the *last sheet* (49th) of the book. The Appendix – *value aspect – in small type* comprises one and a quarter sheets.

Preface ditto returned corrected yesterday. Thus *this volume is finished*. I owe it to YOU solely that this has been possible! Without your self-sacrifice for me I could not possibly have done the enormous work for the 3 volumes. I embrace you, full of thanks!

Enclosed 2 sheets corrected proof.

The 15£ received with best thanks.

Salut, my dear good friend!

Yours, K. Marx

[. . .]

London, 10 October 1867

Dear Fred,

From the enclosed letter from Kugelmann you will see that the time has come for action. You can write to him about my book better than I can myself. At the same time, he is not to be too cumbersome and send us the things for correction but only *after* they have appeared. You must impress on him that everything depends on 'making a noise', much more so than on how or on thoroughness.

---

* The reference is to Karl Marx's *On the Critique of Political Economy* (editor's note).

The enclosed scrap from Meissner contains nothing. How can he expect reviews before his own bookseller's advertisements have appeared?

Salut.

Yours, K. M.

Manchester, 13 October 1867

Dear Moor,

I've written and sent Kugelmann two articles about the book from different points of view; I think they are such that almost any paper can take them, and he can then make others accordingly. That should help him a little.

[. . .]

Yours, F. E.

Manchester, 18 October 1867

Dear Moor,

[. . .]

I can write another 4–5 articles about your book from different points of view but do not know where to send them. Who knows where Siebel is! Maybe in Algiers or Palermo! But I hope to have an answer from him soon. If you could get it copied in London, so that my handwriting cannot be recognized, then it would perhaps be most advisable to send it to Meissner.

Best regards to all.

Yours, F. E.

London, 25 January 1868

Dear Fred,

[. . .]

Concerning *Liebknecht*, there's no need to *butter him up any further*. This young man – as he demonstrated once before in London – is very fond of acting the 'protector'. This is shown also by his last letter to you. He feels very important and if necessary we shall settle our affairs without him and regardless of him. How magnanimous of him that he should print the preface which nearly all papers printed months ago. Or that he arranged for 2 copies of my book to be sent to Contzen and the editor of *Volks-Zeitung* respectively! The best thing would be to show him the cold shoulder. Besides I don't believe that he has read 15 pages of the book yet. After a whole year, whenever it was, he had not yet read *Herr Vogt*, though surely that was no excessively heavy reading matter. His motto is: To teach but not to learn.

[. . .]

Yours, K. Marx

London, 15 February 1868

Dear Fred,

[. . .]

I have received from Bordeaux all the papers for the marriage. It is causing me a great deal of worry. It is to be on 1 April and nothing has yet been properly prepared for Laura. Surely one cannot send her out into the world like a beggar woman. I have written to Holland, but no answer.

[. . .]

Yours, K. M.

Manchester, 20th February 1868

Dear Moor,

You'll have to regard me as totally suspended this week. I have a terrible lot of work in the business as a result of the sudden cotton surcharge, so that I don't get out of the office from morning to 7 o'clock at night and don't get my midday meal until 8 o'clock at night. You'll understand what one is then still capable of doing. I hope that damned carbuncle has cleared up. Warm regards to your wife, the girls and Lafargue.

Yours, F. E.

London, 6 March 1868

Dear Fred,

[...]

I wrote to Holland again yesterday because the matter is getting desperately urgent. Lafargue senior has arranged for the necessary banns, etc., in Bordeaux and has sent all the papers over. He now expects the wedding to be performed early next month and the couple to come to Paris, where he too will arrive later. However, we have not yet dared take the necessary steps about the banns here because my wife has not yet been able to procure even the most necessary things for Laura. The good Freiligrath had everything very easy, but then he is 'noble'.

[...]

Yours, K. M.

London, 25 March 1868

Dear Fred,

I wanted to write to you from the Museum yesterday but I suddenly felt so exceedingly unwell that I had to snap shut the very interesting book I was holding in my hands. It was like a black veil coming down over my eyes. Accompanied by the most terrible headache and tightness in the chest. I therefore sloped off home. The air and the light did me good, and back home I slept for some time. My condition is such that I should really give up all work and thinking for some time; but I *would find that difficult even if I had the means for loafing about.*

[...]

Yours, K. M.

London, 13 August 1868

Dear Fred,

I hope these lines will reach you before your departure because there is danger in delay.

First I must send money to Ramsgate so they can stay another week. Since departure was delayed for weeks after your last consignment some lesser domestic debts were settled, and on the other hand my wife had to collect watches and other things from the pawnshop so she could appear respectable on the bathing beach.

Second one of the grocers who has to receive 6£ and a few shillings must be paid this very week as the fellow is closing his stall.

Third, I have already received 2 summonses for the Queen's taxes (about 8£). The local taxes*, as you know, have been paid. I absolutely cannot put off these items.

[. . .]

Yours, K. M.

Manchester, about 14 August 1868

Dear Moor,

I shall send you some money tomorrow, our cashier has no banknotes left this afternoon. Don't feel embarrassed about 'squeezing' me, I merely wish there was more to be squeezed out, but do consider that in 6 weeks we have to pay the £150 with interest, and Borkheim says the interest brings the matter up to £165!! I think you will have to decide to go to Holland, we cannot afford to borrow at *such* interest rates.

[. . .]

Yours, F. E.

Manchester, 2 October 1868

Dear Moor,

Borkheim has done his business superbly. At the end of last month the item of £72 for wine fell due, which Charles Roesgen, Gumpert and I had obtained from him. But I was only able to make the money liquid at the beginning of this month. I therefore sent it to him yesterday and asked him if he knew of a way of raising £100 for you or if he could leave the wine unpaid for till Feb. He did the latter

* Rates: this is Marx's original English wording (translator's note).

and himself advanced the remaining £28. Thus, I think, we are out of trouble at least for the moment.

But now get on also with the second volume, and get some exercise for your liver.

[. . .]

Yours, F. E.

[. . .]

Manchester, 29 November 1868

Dear Moor,

Consider the answers to the encl. questions *very carefully* and answer them by return so that I get your answer on Tuesday morning.

(1) How much money do you need to pay off *all* your debts so as to have a clear start?

(2) Can you manage on £350 per annum for *ordinary* regular needs (I exclude extra expenditure due to sickness and unforeseen events), i.e. so that you don't have to make any debts. If not, tell me the sum that is necessary. All this assuming that all old debts have previously been paid off. This question of course is the principal question.

The point is that my negotiations with Gottfried Ermen are taking a turn towards him wanting to *buy me out* at the end of my contract – 30 June – i.e., he is offering me a sum of money if I will undertake not to enter into any competitive business for 5 years and permit him to continue running the firm. That's just where I wanted to have the man. But since the balance-sheets have been poor over the past few years I am doubtful whether this offer will enable us to live free from financial worries for a number of years, even presupposing the probable contingency that all kinds of events will get us to remove to the continent again, i.e. additional costs. The sum offered me by Gottfried Ermen (which I had always determined, long before he offered it to me, that it would possibly be used exclusively for covering the necessary subsidy for you) would enable me to transmit to you £350 per annum *reliably* for 5–6 years, and in the event of exceptional contingencies even a little more. But you will realize that all my arrangements would be upset if an amount of debts were again to accumulate from time to time, which would then have to be defrayed from further capital.

Precisely because my calculation must be based on the fact that our maintenance costs will be met not only from *revenue* but also – from the outset – partly from *capital*, precisely because of that it is a little complicated and will have to be strictly adhered to, or else we'll be on the rocks.

It will depend on your answer, in which I request you to describe matters to me as they *really are*, how I proceed *vis-à-vis* Gottfried Ermen. Do therefore yourself determine the sum which you will need regularly each year, and we'll see what can be done.

What will happen after the above-mentioned 5–6 years I cannot myself see clearly as yet. If everything remains the way it is now I would not then, admittedly, be able to transmit to you £350 annually, let alone more, but still always at least £150. But a lot can change by then and your literary work will also help to earn you something.

Best regards to your wife and the girls. Of the encl. photographs send one to Laura.

Yours, F. E.

London, 30 November 1868

Dear Fred,

I am completely knocked down by your all too great kindness.

I got my wife to submit to me all bills, and the sum total of our debts is far greater than I had thought, 210£ (of which approximately 75£ for pawnshop and interest). This calculation does not include the doctor's bill for the treatment during scarlet fever, as he has not yet sent it in.

During the past few years we have needed more than 350£, but the sum is entirely sufficient as (1) Lafargue was living with us during the past few years and expenditure was greatly increased as a result of his presence in the house; (2) everything was paid for much too dearly because of the system of debts. Only by a complete clearance of all debts would I be able to enforce a strict administration.

The fact that little Jenny – behind my back – has engaged herself to *give lessons* in an English family will show you how disagreeable conditions have been at home over the past few months. The business does not start until January 1869. I have subsequently approved the business on condition (the lady of the house, her husband Dr Monroe, came to see my wife about it) that the engagement is *binding for one month only* and either party is *entitled to give notice* after expiry of that month. Distasteful though the matter was to me (the child has to teach small children almost the whole day long) – I don't have to tell you this – still, I agreed on this condition mainly because I thought it good for little Jenny to have her mind taken off things through some occupation and more especially to get her out of our 4 walls. My wife – understandably so in the circumstances but not therefore more agreeable – has for many years lost her mental equilibrium, and with her lamentations and irritability and bad humour plagues the children virtually to death, although no children could take it all in a more jolly way.

But in the end there are certain limits. Of course it is unpleasant to write to you about this. It is easier to say such things. But it is necessary in order to explain to you why I have not absolutely countermanded little Jenny's step.

Yours, K. M.

Marx's (and Engels's) relations with the German labour leaders were by no means unclouded; the fact that Bebel describes a visit to London as a 'journey to Canossa' characterizes the mistrustful and hierarchic distance dividing them. Marx's verdict on Wilhelm Liebknecht was harsh to the point of contempt. As early as in the fifties Marx had called him a solid citizen who was 'as useless as a writer as he is unreliable and a weak character'. This situation remained unchanged through the years, and intensified as Liebknecht in 1862 returned to Germany and worked at building up a party: '... that Schweitzer is right on one point – Liebknecht's incapability ...'; 'Liebknecht has a talent for rallying around him the stupidest people in Germany'; 'Liebknecht has again had the good fortune of fools'. In the end he was referred to as 'that oaf' or 'that solid oaf'.

This is the tone Marx invariably assumed whenever there was personal and political offence. The date of the letter – 16 May 1870 – explains this defamatory sharpness towards a politician whom other contemporaries, such as Eduard Bernstein, credited with unparalleled political talent. In the autumn of the preceding year, Liebknecht and Bebel had succeeded in creating one great political party out of the multiplicity of groups and associations dominating the German socialist scene. At the Eisenach party congress from 7–9 August 1869 – whose temporary venue was called, of all things, 'The Moor' – the Social Democratic Workers' Party of Germany had been founded. This was so repugnant to Marx that the word Eisenach did not occur even once in the letters of that period; even reports on the preparations were grumpily ridiculed and one of Liebknecht's most extensive letters is dismissed with the sentence 'enclosed a letter from little Wilhelm'.

However, it was no longer just mockery of the 'busybody and ignoramus' but a political danger: Liebknecht did not regard Lassalle's followers as the principal enemies and did not fight against them; he even attempted to reach agreement with them. From this moment onwards Liebknecht was invariably snapped at. Although Engels rejected the 'tone of command' – which was not present in Liebknecht's letters – he, for his own part, wrote rather brusquely: 'It seems you are confusing London with Crimmitschau, thinking that a "Citizens' and Peasants' Friend" could be set up here without any difficulty.' Even when Liebknecht amicably offered to give Engels a mandate of the Saxon Social Democrats for the London Conference of the International in September 1871, Engels snapped at him: 'I need no power of attorney'. He, Engels, would be the Delegate of Italy and Spain. Again, Liebknecht had requested Marx and Engels to be godfathers to his son Karl, born on 13 August 1871, and in connection with some document had asked them if they had any other Christian names. Engels penned the harsh reply: 'Marx and I do not deal in secret Christian names, we each have only one.' (This was not true.)

Estrangement and distance are evident. But what the two 'grand old men' were estranged and distant from most was the political scene in Germany. The tone they use towards Liebknecht was also the tone they used towards the German party. Liebknecht had long described it as 'crazy tactics for a workers' party to try and lock itself up in a theoretical castle in the air high above the working people'. He was a practician: he wanted not war with Lassalle's followers but rapprochement, and when the Gotha Party Congress of 1875 eventually witnessed the merger of the two parties to produce the Socialist Workers' Party of Germany this marked the final breach with Marx and Engels. It was then that the now famous Critique of the Gotha Programme *was written, though this remained unpublished during Marx's lifetime.*

London, 14 March 1869

Dear Fred,

[. . .]

Liebknecht has a talent for rallying around him the *stupidest people* in Germany. For instance, the author of 'Democratic Objectives and the German Workers'.* One can only read the stuff if one hears it in one's mind in south German dialect. That oaf requests the workers to get Bismarck off his back and then promises them to satisfy *'full liberality'* and *other* socialist demands! Horror!

[. . .]

Yours, K. M.

Manchester, 18 March 1869

Dear Moor,

I'll write to Meissner about the *Peasant War*.

Wilhelm Liebknecht – also to judge by *Social-Demokraten* (which I'll send you one of these days) – seems to have kept the lead in Saxony. On the other hand one must grant the Lassalleans that they are developing quite a different kind of activity and know how to make ten times more of their limited means than the 'People's Party'. Even during Schweitzer's imprisonment there was no such nonsense in *Soc.-Dem.* as Wilhelm now publishes.

I wonder what Wilhelm has to say to the fact that in Celle the *Hanoverian separatists*, defeated in the first electoral round, voted in the second for the *national-liberal* Bismarck-follower Planck and thereby got him into the Reichstag *against* the worker Yorck! But that won't worry Wilhelm.

[. . .]

Yours, F. E.

---

* This article appeared anonymously in the *Democratic Weekly* on 22 August, 5 September, 21 and 28 November 1868 and 6 March 1869 (editor's note).

London, 20 March 1869

Dear Fred,

[. . .]

I propose to have myself *naturalized* as an Englishman so that I can travel to Paris in safety. Without such a journey a French edition of my book would never come about. My presence there is absolutely necessary. Under Palmerston's law one may again strip off the Englishman after 6 months if one so desires. The law does not protect a naturalized person with regard to offences committed in his native country *prior* to naturalization if he returns to that country. With the exception of this contingency, however, a naturalized subject has equal standing with an Englishman *vis-à-vis* foreign governments. I really don't see why I should not visit Paris *without permission* from Mr Bonaparte if I have a means of doing so.

[. . .]

Yours, Moor
who is increasingly presenting
the picture of a 'white'washed
Moor every day.

Manchester, 6 April 1869

Dear Moor,

Liebknecht has again had the good fortune of fools. The vote of 6,500 against 4,500 was a huge defeat for Schweitzer, even though it was no direct victory for Wilhelm. *Kölner Zeitung* says that Schweitzer was terribly dismayed, and although previously he had declared that he would resign if any appreciable minority voted against him he has nevertheless taken good care not to do so.

Schweitzer's campaign for the tailors' kingdom has certainly foundered and his position in his own association is badly shaken. Not everyone is a dictator who would like to be one. The process of disintegration of specific Lassalleanism has thus set in and is bound to progress rapidly. With 6,500:4,500 there will either be a split or the abandonment of 'tight' organization and of Schweitzer's personal leadership. To that extent Liebknecht's impudence has had a good effect. Nor would I blame him for agreeing to a new armistice

under these circumstances, even though this is now the third instance, between the two of them, of cads' fighting, when ended, is very soon mended.
[...]

Yours, F. E.

London, 15 April 1869

Dear Fred,
[...]
Today I discovered by accident that two *Neveu de Rameau* at home, so am sending you one. The unique masterpiece will give you fresh enjoyment. 'Confusion of mind, aware of itself and declaring itself', old Hegel says about it, 'is derision of existence and of the confusion of the whole and of oneself; it is at the same time the still perceptible dying-away of that entire confusion.... It is the self-disrupting nature of all relationships and the deliberate disruption of them.... On that side of the return into the self the *vanity* of all *things* is its *own vanity*, or else it is vain ... as outraged self-awareness yet it realizes its own confusion, and in this realization it instantly rises above it.... Each part of this world arrives at the point when its spirit is uttered, or that it is spoken of with spirit and that its essence is stated. The *honest awareness* (the role Diderot assigns to himself in the dialogue) accepts each moment as an enduring essence and it is uninformed thoughtlessness not to realize that it equally does the reverse. The confused awareness, however, is the awareness of reversal, moreover of absolute reversal; the concept is the dominant element in it, the element that brings the thoughts together which in honesty lie far apart, and whose language therefore is full of esprit. The content of the language of the spirit of and about itself is likewise the reversal of all concepts and realities, the general deception of speech is therefore the greatest truth.... To the calm awareness, which honestly sets the melody of the good and the true in the identity of tones, i.e. in One Note, this speech appears as "a babble of wisdom and insanity", etc.' [Follows a passage from Diderot].
[...]

Yours, K. M.

139

Manchester, 16 April 1869

Dear Moor,

[. . .]

Many thanks for the *Rameau*, which will give me much enjoyment. I hardly read anything these days in order to get my eye properly well again at long last, I have also cut down on my work at the office.

Wilhelm is greatly mistaken if he thinks I would send him the *Peasant War* in response to such vague phrases – just so he can come again later, screaming that unless I send such and such a sum of money the last sheets cannot be printed. His letter is downright silly and to expect you to pay his fees is downright impudent.

[. . .]

Yours, F. E.

[. . .]

London, 24 April 1869

Dear Fred,

For about 12 days I've been suffering terribly with my old liver complaint. I am guzzling Gumpert's old medicine but so far without success. As a result I am mentally totally paralysed. This condition recurs every spring. If I don't get over it safely the next thing to come is the carbuncles. Will you therefore ask Gumpert if he knows of anything new for me? I haven't smoked for 8 days. That should give you an idea of my condition.

[. . .]

Yours, K. M.

Manchester, 25 April 1869

Dear Moor,

What your liver needs most is a change of air and a change from your customary mode of living. Do the right thing at once therefore, i.e. get into a train at once and come here for 8–14 days. I've taken quite a lot of time off and we shall be able to walk together a good deal. You can also get yourself examined and treated by Gumpert

SELECTED LETTERS

and, on the other hand, because of your 'condition' you'll be able to decline invitations to 'tea'. This will very soon make you invigorated and fit for work again, and you'll then be able to do more work in a few weeks than you would in months in your present condition. Send me a telegram tomorrow morning, at the warehouse, when you get up, what train you'll be coming on, and be here in the evening. That's the simplest and is *certain* to cure you.

Yours, F. E.

London, 26 April 1869

Dear Fred,

Best thanks for the invitation. But it is absolutely impossible for me to travel at this moment. My wife is coughing a lot and I'm waiting therefore; as soon as fit to travel she'll go to Paris, to fetch Tussy. Maybe I'll come over with the latter.

This week, moreover, there are things in the International to be straightened out which won't get straight without me.

Finally, difficult though it is, I've got to finish certain notes as it's always difficult to pick up again, not so much a new subject but in the middle of a certain subject.

With all that, if I don't get any better, I shall of course have to set off.

More tomorrow.

Yours, K. M.

Manchester, 22 June 1869

Dear Moor,

[. . .]

Well, that is a most curious 'Urning' that you've sent me.* These are indeed exceedingly unnatural revelations. The pederasts are beginning to stand up and be counted and discovering that they are a

---

* 'Urning' is a malicious, pejorative word for homosexual, which both Marx and Engels liked to use because they despised and ridiculed homosexuality. Shortly before this letter Marx had sent Engels Karl Heinrich Ulrich's *Argonauticus. Zastrov and the 'Urningen' of the Pietistic, Ultramontane and Free-thinking Camp*, which appeared in Leipzig in 1869. That both of them were occupied with this problem and such reading was connected with the fact that Lassalle's follower, Schweitzer, was homosexual (editor's note).

power in the state. All they lacked was organization, but to judge by this it seems already to exist secretly. And since they include such important men, in all the old and even the new parties, from Rösing to Schweitzer, they cannot fail to be victorious. 'War to the front apertures, peace to the rear apertures of the body', will be the slogan now.† It is fortunate that we personally are too old to have to worry that, at the victory of this party, we might have to pay physical tribute to the victors. But the young generation! Incidentally, only in Germany is it possible that a chap comes along and transforms this filth into a theory and then invites: Join us, etc. Unfortunately he still lacks the courage to declare himself openly as 'that' and still has to operate before the public 'from the front' though not, as he says in one place, by a slip, 'in from the front'. But just wait till the new North German Criminal Code recognizes the rights of the posterior, then he'll talk quite differently. And we poor frontal chaps, with our childish inclination towards women, we'll have a very thin time then. If that man Schweitzer were any use he might lure this strange solid citizen into disclosing the identities of those prominent and most prominent pederasts – which surely should not be difficult for him as a kindred spirit.
[. . .]

Yours, F. E.

Manchester, 1 July 1869

Dear Moor,

Hurray! Today sweet commerce is at an end, and I am a free man. Also I settled all the main points with our good Gottfried yesterday; he yielded all along the line. Tussy and I have today celebrated my first day of freedom by taking a long walk through the fields. And my eye is a lot better and with a little care will no doubt soon be in tip-top condition.
[. . .]

Yours, F. E.

† Allusion to the French Revolution slogan: 'War to the palaces, peace to the cottages!' (translator's note).

London, 3 July 1869

Dear Fred,

Warmest congratulations on your exodus from Egyptian bondage!

In honour of this event I drank a 'glass beyond thirst', but late at night and not, as the Prussian gendarmes, before sunrise.

Enclosed a weighty letter from Wilhelm. You will see from it that he has suddenly appointed himself my *Curator* and is prescribing for me this, that and the other thing that I MUST do.

I *must* come to their August Congress, *must* show myself to the German workers; *must* send the international cards *immediately* (not having had a reply from them for 3 months in spite of two enquiries), *must* re-fuck the *Communist Manifesto*! must come to Leipzig!

Is it not the height of naivity that in the same letter in which he deplores *not* being able to return to me the 2 £ (which I assigned for him to Eccarius) he offers *me my travelling expenses* to Germany! He doesn't change!

About you he seems to be morally indignant. I have already answered him that he has misinterpreted your letter. The man simply cannot understand that opinions and business management are by no means diametrically opposed, as he assumes with his newspaper management, and as others, too, have to assume unless they want to become suspects.

Our Wilhelm is a sanguine type and a liar. Thus probably again considerable exaggeration in the account of his victory over Schweitzer. But there's certainly something to it. Schweitzer would not have been reconverted to the Hatzfeldt church if his position in his own association had not been shaken. On the other hand he accelerated the general dissolution by the clumsy staging of his final coup d'état. I hope that as a result of this affair the German workers' movement will at last leave the stage of that infantile complaint of Lassalleanism and that any remnant of it will perish in mere sectarian isolation.

As for the various 'absolute commandments' of Wilhelm, I have answered him to this effect:

I feel no urge whatever to show myself to the German workers and shall *not* come to their Congress. Once they have really joined the 'International' and given themselves a decent party organization – and the Nuremberg Congress has shown how little faith should be placed in mere promises, tendencies, etc. – some opportunity will arise by and by. At the same time it must be clearly understood that the new organization must not be to us either a 'People's Party' nor a Lassallean church. If we came now we would surely have to speak *against the People's Party*, and that would not please Wilhelm or Bebel! And if – miraculously – they were to admit this themselves, surely we would have to throw *our weight* onto the scales against Schweitzer and Associates instead of having the overturn appear as the free action of the workers themselves.

As for rejigging the *Manifesto*, we would consider that as soon as we have seen the resolutions of their Congress, etc.

He should keep his 2£ and not worry about my travelling expenses. I commend their stand against Becker.

[. . .]

El Moro

London, 22 July 1869

Dear Fred,

[. . .]

[. . .] I shall 'shake off' Herr Wilhelm if he involves me in a mess for a third time. The fellow has not even got the excuse of going with us through thick and thin. He commits his stupidities off his own bat, tells us about them whenever he sees fit, and identifies us with him whenever he can see no other way out.

For about 6 days I've had a fierce carbuncle on my left arm, which is not pleasant in 'this heat'.

I had yet another 'familial' unpleasantness. The point is that for some time I've noticed that my wife is not managing with the money I give her each week, even though our expenses have in no way increased. As I certainly don't wish to get into debt again, and as the money that I gave her last Monday was again all 'gone' yesterday, I asked for an explanation. And then the folly of women emerged. In the list of debts which I made her compile for you she had suppressed approximately 75£ which she was now trying to pay off bit by bit from the housekeeping money. I asked her why? Answer: She was afraid to come out with the big overall total! Women evidently always need some guardianship!

[. . .]

Yours, Moor

[. . .]

Manchester, 25 July 1869

Dear Moor,

Don't lose any sleep over the £75; as soon as Gottfried pays me my next instalment, i.e. as soon as the balance-sheet is done and the contracts are signed, I'll send it to you. Just make sure nothing of the kind happens again in future. As you know, our calculation is very tightly made and leaves absolutely no margin for extravagances. I too have been keeping accounts of all expenses since 1 July in order to see what the whole lot is costing me and in order to know where to make cuts if necessary.

[. . .]

The impudence of our good Wilhelm really surpasses the limit.* Actually trying to prove to you that with his lie he was keeping 'within the boundaries of your letter'! How rotten his conscience was is proved by the fact that he uses the term 'take account of', normally so hateful to him, and by his final sentimental appeal to your kind heart. This moron expects us and the entire International to follow him through all his about-turns in the matter of Schweitzer, to make peace when he makes peace, to hit out at Schweitzer when he hits out, and moreover to allow him to tell lies right and left in the name of the International whenever he considers it 'necessary'. And *he* wants to prescribe to the Congress who is to be admitted and who isn't.

A good thing *he* 'conceded' to you the defence in the Vogt business, and 'for party considerations'. The man really regards himself as someone important.

[. . .]

Yours, F. E.

---

* Wilhelm Liebknecht was carrying on what Marx understood to be a 'high-handed battle' with Lassalle's follower Schweitzer. On 22 July 1869, in reply to a letter from Marx which has since been lost, Liebknecht repudiated these accusations and said: 'I concede that I am acting high-handedly – when one is involved in a battle, one always behaves high-handedly or not at all.' Another point is that J. B. von Schweitzer professed to be a friend of Marx's, which Liebknecht thought politically intolerable; as it also says in the letter referred to: 'You surely don't want to be seen in the eyes of the German workers as this scoundrel's patron?' (editor's note).

Manchester, 17 November 1869

Dear Moor,

I hope the arsenic and the movement will have commanded a thunderous 'Back – at the double!' to the 'disquieting' you-know-what. But equally I hope that from these ever-recurring relapses you will at last conclude that a more sensible way of life must be embarked upon. You yourself are poisoning your blood by rendering a regular digestion impossible for yourself. And in consequence I am sure you don't accomplish the same quantum (or quality) of work that you would accomplish under more normal circumstances. [. . .]

Yours, F.E.

Manchester, 19 November 1869

Dear Moor,

[. . .]

Even before your letter of yesterday arrived I had sent Wilhelm £5 with a few cool lines. That man really is too impudent. First he insults me in every possible way and then I am to support him spiritually and materially, send him articles for his rag which, without so much as a word, he has stopped sending me. If you write to him you will oblige me by making it clear to him that if he wants articles from me he should be good enough to write to me direct. To be Herr Wilhelm's shoeblack – what next! Am returning the letters enclosed. [. . .]

Yours, F.E.

[. . .]

Manchester, 19 January 1870

Dear Moor,

I hope you are better again with that infamous carbuncle after lancing it. But it is a hideous business. Why don't you stick with the arsenic until all symptoms have disappeared and *then for at least another 3 months.* I shall go and see Gumpert one of these days and ask his opinion, but please let me know beforehand how long you suspended the arsenic and when you resumed again so that I can answer his very first question.

I should have thought that you would really have realized by now that even in the interests of your 2nd volume it is necessary for you to change your way of life. With this perpetual recurrence of interruptions you'll never finish it; with increased exercise in fresh air, which will keep the carbuncles away, you'll finish sooner or later.

Unfortunately, now that I can no longer give orders to the packers in the warehouse, I don't have the facilities for sending wine as before. I have to wait, as I did with the Brauneberger, until I find a ready-packed case, or otherwise depend on chance. That is also why the small case of port wine which I'm sending you today has turned out so thin. It is an old butter crate of Renshaw's, and I couldn't get more than 5 bottles into the narrow space; besides the thin boards wouldn't have stood a greater weight. Still, no doubt it will keep you going for some time.

[...]

Yours, F. E.

London, 27 January 1870

Dear Fred,

I am still under treatment and under house arrest. The business was somewhat complicated by small carbuncles in the vicinity of the abscess, which was nearly the size of an egg. But in a few days all will be quite right.

Odd how physicians differ in their opinions. Dr Maddison, who held a post in a skin disease hospital in Edinburgh and still looks after this speciality in a London hospital alongside his practice, says that in both hospitals they are totally *against arsenic* for carbuncles but in favour of arsenic for skin rash. While I am under his care, which comes to an end this week, I am of course taking *his* medicine. As soon as this is over I shall take the arsenic regularly for 3 months because this has got to finish.

Enclosed the earlier-mentioned note from Wilhelm. When you write to him you might tell him by the way (with reference to the enclosed scrap to me) (1) that, if all journals discuss the *18th Brumaire* as much as his, which is not at all, then it is not surprising that no one hears about it; (2) that, if (I think it's humbug) the thing is unobtainable in Leipzig, then surely one should write off for it not to me but *direct to Meissner*.

[. . .]

Yours, K. M.

Marx's relationship with the Russian anarchist-revolutionary Bakunin – who had to flee from Dresden in 1848 in the same stage coach as Richard Wagner, and whose correspondence with Marx headed Arnold Ruge's German–French Annals, and to whom, more recently, Ricarda Huch devoted a biographical essay – was, similar to his relationship with Lassalle, confused and full of contradictions. The statement made about Bakunin by the revolutionary Police President during the Lyons Commune might well be a remark by Marx: 'What a man! On the first day of a revolution he is a veritable treasure; on the second he should be shot.'

For Marx the 'first day' was the day of the foundation of the International, the consummation of his political life. That was the moment when he wrote to Engels 'Bakunin sends his regards' – and this referred to their first meeting in sixteen years. Six weeks previously Marx had written a letter of condolence to Countess Hatzfeldt on Lassalle's death, three days previously he had presented his 'inaugural address' to the committee of that 'International Workers' Assembly' in London's St Martin's Hall. The encounter with Bakunin should be seen in this historical context – an encounter whose accomplishment had been uncertain for decades ('... We are at present making suits for the great Bakunin ...', we read in a letter from his friend Lessner). The two men had the same tailor, and thus a meeting came about which was important to Marx; that very day he called on his former (and future) opponent.

As early as July 1848 Marx had published a brief denunciation in Neue Rheinische Zeitung *to the effect that Bakunin was a Russian spy and an agent of the Tsar. The source of this report – 'it hit me on the head like a roof tile', Bakunin said – was alleged to be George Sand, but she denied this at once. Marx never shook off this shadow of the denunciator. Nor was Bakunin ever prepared to regard this as a journalistic slip; instead he saw it as the expression of Marx's despotically autocratic character which refused to tolerate divergent political* views, a 'red Bismarck', whose theory of 'governing, educating and organizing' the masses in accordance with his own 'idea' he fought against: 'Marx has the passionate desire of seeing his ideas, the proletariat, and with it his own self, win victory.'

The tangle of emigré existence resulted in the next 'incident' – to which Marx alludes in letters to Engels – being ascribed to Marx, but in fact it had nothing to do with him. While Bakunin languished in Siberian prisons an article appeared in a London newspaper in 1853, once again suspecting him of espionage for Russia. The article was signed F. M., the initials of a man called Marx. Except that it was a different Marx: the accusation in the Morning Advertiser came from a landowner named Francis Marx. However, nobody was prepared to believe this. A mere two days later the paper, which was close to the reactionary English politician David Urquhart – these are 'Urquhart's denunciations' – published a letter from Ruge (who had meanwhile also become an enemy of Marx) recalling the earlier infamy of 1848.

This was the issue when Marx visited Bakunin in London in 1864 and this was also what Bakunin referred to when he said, 'I knew he was telling me an untruth.' Bakunin remained convinced that Marx was once more after his honour and his life, especially as the Morning Advertiser had not published Marx's disclaimer.

The two men differed as much in their character as in their political concepts. Bakunin, who regarded Marx as a pan-German emperor, himself wanted to abolish the state and suspected that Marx merely wanted a new state, a state-organized socialism under Prussian-German hegemony. That is why Bakunin in 1868 founded the 'Alliance de la Démocratie Socialiste' in Geneva as the international organization of anarchists – clearly directed against the International. Marx called the Alliance 'that shit', full of 'idéalisme russe', and persecuted Bakunin with a variety of public and discreet harassments. He regarded this anarchist counter-organization as a danger to the International, the more so as Bakunin was meeting with a considerable echo in the Latin countries, especially in Italy. Marx picked up every possible rumour, whether about irregular financial matters or alleged addresses of loyalty from Bakunin to the Tsar, and used them in his struggle against his opponent until Bakunin finally withdrew to Locarno in 1874, too poor to buy a cup of tea and full of 'hatred against revolutionary propaganda as conducted by Marx'.

At the Hague Congress of the International Marx made a personal *appearance and submitted allegedly incriminating documents. Bakunin was 'annihilated': he was expelled and sent what Engels called the 'notice of his political death', to the* Journal de Genève: *'I am retiring – from now on I shall no longer trouble anyone, and I ask nothing except that I am left alone.'*

London, 10 February 1870

Dear Fred,

[. . .]

[. . .] The entire Bakunin band has left *'Egalité'*. Bakunin himself has set up his residence in the Ticino and will continue his intrigues in Switzerland, Spain, Italy and France. Between us the armistice is now over since he knows that, on the occasion of the latest Geneva events, I forcefully attacked and denounced him. The oaf really imagines we are *'too bourgeois'* and hence incapable of comprehending or appreciating his sublime conceptions of 'hereditary right', 'equality' and the replacement of the existing political system by *'L'Internationale'*. In name his *'Alliance* de la Démocratie Socialiste' is abolished but in fact it persists [. . .]

[. . .]

K. M.

Manchester, 11 February 1870

Dear Moor,

[. . .]

[. . .] It's a good thing Bakunin has gone to the Ticino. He won't do much harm there, and surely it is proof that the Geneva business is over. Since such ambitious vain incompetents exist in every movement it is basically a good thing for them to rally in their own way and then to come out into the open with their world-shaking crankinesses. It can then soon be shown to the whole world that it is all just so much puff. And that is preferable to having the struggle remain in the area of private gossip, where people who have a job to do are never a match for those who have the entire day for clever speculation. But one's got to keep a sharp eye on the blighters so they don't without opposition occupy territory in some place or another. Spain and Italy, admittedly, one will have to concede to them, at least for the moment.

[. . .]

Yours, F. E.

London, 19 February 1870

Dear Fred,

[. . .]

At last an article in Katkov's paper in which he suspects Bakunin (1) of certain financial affairs, (2) describes him as his Siberian correspondent and (3) accuses him of having written, either from Siberia or shortly before his relegation there – I cannot remember exactly – an exceedingly *submissive letter to the Emperor Nicholas.* Borkheim is going to send me a copy of it which I will then communicate to you.

[. . .]

Yours, K. M.

[. . .]

Manchester, 22 February 1870

Dear Moor,

[. . .]

Things have become quite intolerable with Monsieur Wilhelm. You will have seen how 'owing to the absence of the typesetter' (who therefore is the real editor) the *Peasant War* is being printed in a mix-up such as Grandperret could not improve upon and yet the oaf has the nerve to add marginal glosses without any reference to their author, glosses which are pure nonsense and which *everyone is bound to ascribe to me.* I have objected to it once before and he acted piqued; but now the nonsense is so thick on the ground that it is no longer a joke. The man's gloss on Hegel is: known to the broader public as the discoverer (sic) and glorifier (sic!) of the royal Prussian *idea of the state* (sic!!). I have now appropriately reacted to this and sent him a statement, as mild as possible in the

151

circumstances, for publication. This oaf, who has for years help-lessly ridden the ridiculous conflict between right and might rather like an infantry man put on a horse with staggers and locked up in an arena – this ignoramus now has the impertinence to try and dismiss a fellow like Hegel with the word 'Prussian' and moreover persuade the public that *I* have said this. I am sick of the business. If Wilhelm does not publish my statement I shall approach his superior, the 'Executive Committee', and if they too try their tricks I'll forbid further printing. Better not be published at all than be proclaimed an ass through Wilhelm's printing.
[...]

Yours, F. E.

London, 16 May 1870

Dear Fred,
[...]
I wrote to that solid oaf Wilhelm straight away and gave him a good piece of my mind. Also pointed out that his remarks about you are 'too childish' to deserve an answer. He could however rely on it that his (Wilhelm's) 'private views on Hegel or anything else' were a matter of complete indifference to you, likewise the circumstance 'which' or 'how many kinds of essays' he (Wilhelm) was 'a little contemptuous of'. The fellow's assertion that he has led a 'restless life for 22 years, ruling out any leisure' is quite delicious. We know that of the 22 years he spent approximately 15 doing nothing.
[...]

Yours, K. M.

The final section of this selected correspondence seems dispro-portionately short. This is due to the circumstance that, for one thing, Engels had been living in London since the autumn of 1870 so that the correspondence was confined to insignificant everyday trifles, and, for another, to Marx's steadily deteriorating health – virtually a protracted early death.

For the last years of his life Marx was a broken, gravely suffering man, travelling from watering place to seaside resort, from one health resort to another. The touching, despairing, human, increasingly gentle letters (for the first time, e.g. in the letters from Algeria, there appear descriptions of scenery) are of scarcely any historical significance except for the scholar interested in the minutest detail. Even Marx's German became increasingly confused; thus in May 1882 he wrote: 'Mon cher, you like other family members, will have mistakes in my orthography, construction, wrong grammar noticed; always notice them – with my still very absent-mindedness – only post festum.' This was an Ahasver-like blind wandering of a lonely man – after all, he had always tried to keep even Engels at a slight distance, and now still wrote: 'Good old Fred may easily kill someone out of love.' Escape to Algiers brought not sunshine and sea breezes but cold and rain, throughout the two and a half spring months. Only the very last weeks were warm enough for Marx to have his hair cut short and – for the first, only and last time in his life – have his beard shaved off entirely. The whole journey, with its oriental fairy-tale character, was faintly unreal: the leisurely first-class voyage by a 'paquebot à vapeur des Postes Françaises' from Marseilles; the stay at the exclusive hotel 'd'Orient' (later to become the Algiers City Hall); the entire exotic backcloth.

From Algeria, no better at all, Marx went to Monte Carlo for four weeks. In the early summer he moved to Argenteuil, to the Longuet family; then to the sulphur spa of Enghien; then, with his daughter Laura, to Vevey on Lake Geneva for six weeks.

Back in London Marx was only temporarily improved. Fog and wet weather again drove him to Ventnor on the Isle of Wight – where he found more fog and wet weather. Endless solitary walks made him more sick and more melancholic. There was no thought of work. The final blow: Jenny Longuet, his first-born and mother of his only grandchild, died on 11 January, at the age of 38. Eleanor scarcely knew how to break the news to him: 'I felt that I was bringing my father his death warrant. On the long sad journey I had tortured my brain to discover how to break the news to him. I did not have to break it to him, my face betrayed me. Moor said at once: "Our little Jenny is dead!" '

Marx had lost his will to live. Laryngitis, bronchitis, an ulcer on the lung – he now bore everything with stoic equanimity. He suffered mustard baths to be prepared for his cold feet; with revulsion he drank the hated warm milk, a litre a day with a quarter bottle of brandy. He became thinner every day. The last extant letter to Engels, two months before his death, concludes: 'Yet I hope with patience and pedantic self-control to get back on the rails again soon. The Moor.' Reassuring doctors allowed Engels to hope that there was a good prospect of getting Marx back on his feet. Three days later he stood in front of the famous armchair. Karl Marx was dead.

London, 30 August 1873

Dear Fred,

[...]

Yesterday, a few hours before writing to you, I had one more narrow escape, but I can still feel it in my bones today. I took a spoonful of raspberry vinegar, some of which got into my windpipe. I had a veritable choking spasm, face quite black, etc., another fraction of a second and I would have left this world. What occurred to me afterwards: could one not produce such accidents artificially? It would be the most decent and least suspicious manner, and yet very quick, for a man to make his own exit from the world. One would be doing the English a great service by publicly recommending such experiments.

[...]

Yours, K. M.

[...]

Karlsbad, 1 September 1874

Dear Fred,

Next Wednesday I shall have been here two weeks, and my powder, alias money, will just about stretch to a third week. If you write to me do so please at the above address, but to Miss Eleanor Marx on the envelope. The treatment has done Tussy wonderfully well; I am feeling better but my insomnia is not yet under control.

We are both living strictly according to the regime. Mornings at 6 o'clock at the various springs, where I have to drink seven glasses. Between every two glassfuls always 15 minutes of marching up and down; after the last glass a walk of one hour, eventually coffee. At night before going to bed one more cold glassful.

I am now restricted to Chateau Pump, that profane beverage; Tussy, on the other hand, receives one glass of Pilsen beer daily, on which I cast jealous eyes. My doctor, prescribed to me by Kugelmann, an Austrian who in manner, speech, etc., resembles the famous General Cecilia, was at first not without anxiety about my sojourn. On his advice I am registered as *Charles* Marx, *independent means*, London, the *'independent means'* resulting in my having to pay double *spa tax* to the worthy city exchequer, both for myself and Eleanor, but having avoided the suspicion that I might be the notorious Karl Marx. However, yesterday I was denounced as just that man in the Vienna gossip paper *Sprudel* (spa journal), and the Polish patriot Count Plater (a good Catholic, a liberal aristocrat) alongside me as 'chief of the Russian nihilists'. But this comes probably too late now since I possess a receipt from the town for spa tax paid. I could also have lived much more cheaply than where Kugelmann arranged for me, though this was useful in my specific circumstances, and perhaps even necessary, because of its air of respectability. *On no account*, although Kugelmann does not know yet, shall I return via Hanover, but will instead take the southerly route by which I arrived. The man annoys me with his emotional nagging – or the rudeness with which he needlessly makes his own and his family's lives miserable. It is possible, on the other hand, that I may have to stay in Karlsbad for five weeks.

The surroundings here are very beautiful, and one never gets tired of walking through or over the wooded granite mountains. But no birds inhabit these forests. The birds are healthy and have no love of the mineral vapours.

I hope that dear Jenny has recovered a little.

Best regards to all from

The Moor

London, 5 September 1874

Dear Moor,

[...]

That the treatment should initially have intensified your sleeplessness seems to be normal in view of the unavoidably stimulating effect of the waters. If you keep your physician posted on that symptom he will adjust his prescriptions accordingly and see to it that this business does not reach too serious a degree.

Jenny wrote to Tussy this week – I think Tuesday or Wednesday – the letter will no doubt have arrived.

Jenny has experienced no after-effects of the tour of the caves so that even a drive through two hours of rain in an open carriage last Tuesday – we were caught out by the weather on our drive home – passed without incident. Besides, she was well protected by umbrella, rainwear and scarf. But all in all we had continually fine weather these past few days whereas the continent is said to have had unholy rain.

Jersey has changed a great deal since we were there together. A vast amount of building, elegant villas, big hotels – high, almost English, prices in them, everything also much more expensive in the market. Here, too, the London market has a price-raising effect. The French language rapidly disappearing, even the country children now speak almost nothing but English amongst themselves, and the people under 30 speak English without any French accent, nearly all of them. Only the elderly distinguished citizens still cling firmly to French. There are now also 2 railways there, and on these you hardly ever hear a word of French. During the season there are daily excursions through the island by five different entrepreneurs. On one occasion we joined one of over 150 persons in 8–9 carriages, the public – philistines, commercial clerks and volunteers, and snobs – giving rise to some amusement and occasional annoyance. The true Briton casts off his cultivated manner as soon as he is on such a trip in Jersey, but resumes it the more conscientiously at the table d'hôte. The increasing availability of money among certain rising individuals – one can hardly call them strata – of England's small middle class and the resulting extent of luxury and of refined so-called good society was easy to observe in Jersey just because Jersey is still regarded as an inexpensive and hence unfashionable little island. The respectability standards of Jersey visitors seem to decline each year – but we made the same observation also in Ramsgate, where no one complained about this more vociferously than the unfortunate barber who cut our hair so short last April.

[...]

Yours, General

[...]

Karlsbad, 18 September 1874

Dear Fred,

We're off on Monday; our route lies via Leipzig, where I shall stop a while and see Wilhelm, and then to Hamburg.

You know that I am a very lazy correspondent; but that was not the reason for my stubborn silence this time. Spent the first three weeks almost sleepless; this, together with the exertions here, will explain everything.

Although one drinks the waters only in the morning (in the evening, before going to bed, one has a cold glass from a special spring brought to one's house), one is nevertheless all day long in a kind of machine which leaves one virtually with not a free moment.

Up at 5 o'clock or half-past 5 in the morning. Then 6 glassfuls taken in succession at different springs. Between each glassful and the next there must be at least 15 minutes.

Then you prepare for breakfast, to start with by buying the rolls that go with the treatment. After that a brisk walk of at least an hour, finally coffee, which is excellent here, at one of the cafés outside the town. Next follows a tour on foot through the surrounding hills; roughly at 12 noon one gets back home but every other day one also takes a bath, which again takes up an hour.

Follows a change of clothing, then lunch at some hostelry or other.

To sleep *after* the meal is strictly forbidden (before the meal it's permitted), and rightly so as I convinced myself the only time I tried it. So another walk to be taken, alternating with carriage drives, return to Karlsbad 6–8 o'clock at night, a light evening snack, and – to bed. As a variation the theatre (which always closes at 9 o'clock, like all other entertainments), concert, reading-room.

Because of the effect of the waters one's head here gets very irritable; you will understand therefore that Kugelmann became unbearable to me in the long run. For convenience he had given me a room between his own and Tussy's, so·that I had the pleasure of his company not only when I was together with him but also when I was on my own. His persistent serious platitudinous babble, uttered in a deep voice, I bore patiently; less so the Hamburg-Bremen-Hanoverian pack of philistines, male and female, who never let go of one; in the end I lost my temper when he annoyed me rather too much with his domestic scenes. This arch-pedantic, bourgeois philistine with his petty interests is actually convinced that his wife does not understand or comprehend his Faustian nature with its soaring into higher philosophy, and he torments the little lady, who is in every respect his superior, in the most repugnant manner. As a result there was a row between us; I moved up to a higher floor, altogether emancipated myself from him (he had seriously ruined my treatment) and we did not get reconciled until just before his departure (which was last Sunday). But I declared positively that I would not inflict myself on him in Hanover.

Quite a pleasant person to talk to was Simon Deutsch (the one I had that row with in Paris and who called on me here at once); besides, half the local medical faculty soon clustered around me and my daughter; all of them most suitable people for my purposes here, where one should reflect little and laugh a lot. The painter Knille from Berlin also a very charming fellow.

Some enjoyable details about my adventures with that Hans Heiling Kugelmann to be left till London.

The more details one hears 'out of Austria', the more one becomes convinced that that state is nearing its end.

I have so far lost 4 pounds (avoirdupois) and can feel with my own hand that my liver steatosis is disappearing. I believe that in Karlsbad I have at last achieved my purpose, at least for a year. I shall be very pleased to find a few lines from you in Hamburg at Meissner's.

With best regards from Tussy and me to Madame Lizzy and Pumps.

Yours, Moor

[...]

Ramsgate, 19 July 1877

Dear Moor,

[...]

Our misfortune is only that our people in Germany have such pitiful opponents. If on the side of the bourgeoisie there were even a single one capable and economically informed head he would very soon put the gentlemen in their places and lead them to clarity about their own confusion. But what can come out of a struggle where both on this side and on the other the weapons are merely platitudes and philistine piffle! Facing those superior bourgeois brains in Germany a new German vulgarized socialism is developing which proves a worthy successor to the old 'true socialism' of 1845.

[...]

Yours, F. E.

Chronological Table

Compiled from: *Karl Marx – A Chronicle of his Life in Separate Dates*, Moscow 1934 (reprinted Frankfurt, n.d.) and other sources.

5 May 1818	Karl Marx born in Trier, Brückergasse 664 (now Brückenstrasse 10), the son of the lawyer Heinrich Marx and his wife Henriett, *née* Pressburg.
26 August 1824	Marx's father – himself baptised as early as *c.* 1816 – has his children Sophie, Karl, Hermann, Henriette, Luise, Emilie and Karoline baptized Protestants.
15 October 1835	Enrolment at University of Bonn.
Late August–Mid-October 1836	Marx spends his summer vacations in Trier. Secret engagement to Jenny von Westphalen, daughter of Government Counsellor Ludwig von Westphalen.
Mid-October 1836	Journey to Berlin. On 22 October Marx is enrolled in the Faculty of Law of Berlin University.
6 April 1841	Marx submits his doctoral thesis on 'The Difference between Democritean and Epicurean Natural Philosophy' to Professor Bachmann, the Dean of the Faculty of Philosophy in the University of Jena.
15 April 1841	Marx receives his doctorate from the Faculty of Philosophy in the University of Jena.
Mid-October 1842	Marx moves to Cologne and on 15 October assumes the editorship of *Rheinische Zeitung*.
c. 24 November 1842	Marx briefly makes Engels's acquaintance when the latter, en route for England, calls at the editorial office of *Rheinische Zeitung*.
17/18 March 1843	Marx formally relinquishes the editorship of *Rheinische Zeitung* and publishes a 'statement' that he has left the editorial board 'because of the present censorship conditions'.
19 June 1843	Marriage to Jenny von Westphalen.
Late October 1843	Marx moves to Paris; lives at 38 rue Vaneau in the Faubourg St Germain.

Late December 1843	Ruge introduces Marx to Heine, from when onwards Marx remains in lively personal contact with him throughout his time in Paris.
c. March 1844	Marx and Engels, having both become contributors to *Deutsch-Französische Jahrbücher* (*German-French Annals*), enter into correspondence with each other.
1 May 1844	Marx's first child is born – his daughter Jenny.
c. July 1844	Marx makes personal contact with Proudhon, keeps in close personal touch with him throughout the rest of his stay in Paris and 'in the course of lengthy, often all-night, discussions infects' him 'with Hegelianism'.
August–December 1844	Marx frequently meets Bakunin.
c. 28 August– *c.* 6 September 1844	Engels, returning to Germany from England, calls on Marx in Paris and spends ten days with him; it is during that period that their 'agreement in all theoretical fields became obvious and our joint work dates from then'.
2 February 1845	Together with Heinrich Bürgers Marx travels via Liège to Brussels, where he is shortly afterwards joined by his wife and daughter.
Late February 1845	Publication in Frankfurt of *The Holy Family, or Critique of Critical Critique. Against Bruno Bauer and Associates. By Friedrich Engels and Karl Marx.*
c. early April 1845	Engels moves from Barmen to Brussels to be near Marx. It is at this meeting that Marx introduces him to 'the materialist theory of history, worked out complete in its main lines'.
c. 12 July– *c.* 21 August 1845	Marx and Engels make a study trip to England, where they make contact in London with the League of the Just and with Weitling.
September 1845	Marx's daughter Laura is born.
December 1845	Marx has himself released from Prussian citizenship.
15 August 1846	Engels moves to Paris in order to engage in propaganda and organizational work on behalf of the Brussels Communist Correspondence Committee.
Early June 1847	First Congress of the League of Communists in London. For lack of money, among other things, Marx cannot travel to London and gets Engels (from Paris) and W. Wolff (from Brussels) to represent him. The Congress resolves to reorganize the League of the Just totally, to assume the name 'League of Communists' and to prepare a Communist Creed for the next Congress.
Early July 1847	Marx's polemical pamphlet *The Poverty of Philosophy. A Reply to Proudhon's Philosophy of Poverty* is published in 800 copies by C. G. Vogler in Brussels – Marx's first economic essay to be printed.

29 November– c. 10 December 1847	Marx participates in the second Congress of the League of Communists in London, which adopts the programmatic and tactical principles championed by Marx and Engels in prolonged discussions, and instructs Marx to draft the Manifesto of the Communist Party.
c. late January 1848	Marx completes the manuscript of the *Manifesto of the Communist Party* and sends it to London to be printed.
Late February 1848	The *Manifesto of the Communist Party* is published in London.
c. 25 February– c. 4 March 1848	Marx takes an active part in the preparations for an armed republican uprising in Brussels. He donates major sums of money to arming the local workers. He also participates in the preparations for an armed uprising in Cologne.
4 March 1848	Marx is arrested by the police at 1 am while getting ready to leave; after several hours of detention he is released and taken under police escort to the French frontier, whence he immediately continues his journey to Paris.
c. 10 March 1848	The central authority of the League of Communists constitutes itself in Paris, elects Marx its President, Schapper its Secretary, and Bauer, Engels (then still in Brussels), Moll, Wallau and W. Wolff as members.
10/11 April 1848	On 10 April Marx arrives in Cologne with Engels and Dronke and at once assumes organization of a big daily, *Neue Rheinische Zeitung*, started by democratic and partially communist groupings.
31 May–1 June 1848	On the evening of 31 May the first issue of *Neue Rheinische Zeitung – an Organ of Democracy* is published – under the date of 1 June – with the announcement (repeated several times in subsequent issues) of the editorial committee below the masthead: 'Karl Marx, editor-in-chief; Heinrich Bürgers, Ernst Dronke, Wilhelm Wolff – editors.' Because of an article by Engels published in this first issue, criticizing the Frankfurt National Assembly, a large number of shareholders sever their links with the paper.
25 September 1848	On the strength of a state of emergency proclaimed at noon, printing of *Neue Rheinische Zeitung*, which had already begun, is suspended in the afternoon and the paper prohibited until further notice.
13 October 1848	Following the end of the state of emergency on 3 October *Neue Rheinische Zeitung* is published again with No. 114 dated 13 October. At the masthead Marx announces that the editorial board remains unchanged and that Freiligrath has joined it as a new member.
9 May 1849	The government in Cologne issues an expatriation order against Marx. The order is served on Marx on 16 May.

18 May 1849	The last issue of *Neue Rheinische Zeitung* (No. 301) is published, printed in red, in several editions, and many thousands of copies are distributed over the next few days.
c. 3 June 1849	Arrival in Paris.
24 August 1849	Marx leaves Paris and – leaving his family behind there for the moment – goes to London.
5 November 1849	Marx's second son, Guido, is born.
c. 10 November 1849	Engels arrives in London after a five weeks' voyage from Genoa.
1850	For most of the year Marx is most intensively engaged on the organizational and political management of financial support for the German refugees in London.
Early March 1850	The first issue of *Neue Rheinische Zeitung – Political-Economic Review* is published in Hamburg in 2,500 copies. From Marx the issue contains the article on 'The Defeat of June 1848' – 'Marx's first attempt to interpret a piece of contemporary history in the light of his materialist philosophy from the economic situation prevailing at the time' (Engels).
1850	Because of his arrears with his rent Marx's last domestic chattels are pawned and the family forcibly evicted. They move into a German hotel at 1 Leicester Street, Leicester Square.
c. May 1850	Marx enters into contact with representatives of the 'decidedly revolutionary party' of Hungary and makes the acquaintance of, among others, Stephan Türr and Johann Bangya (an Austrian police spy).
c. 13 May 1850	Marx moves to 64 Dean Street, Soho Square, into a two-room flat; in December moves to 28 Dean Street.
c. mid-May 1850	Marx makes the acquaintance of Wilhelm Liebknecht, recently expelled from Switzerland, on a country outing of the German Workers Association.
Mid-June 1850	Marx is given access to the British Museum Reading Room.
c. late August 1850	Marx plans to emigrate to America in November with his family, and together with Engels. He instructs Rothacker, who is travelling there, to prepare the ground with friends and acquaintances in New York, and in particular to explore the prospects of founding a newspaper.
Late September 1850	Marx resumes his great theoretical economic work planned ever since 1844 – a critique of political economy. He is a regular visitor to the British Museum and reads and makes excerpts there.
19 November 1850	Marx's son Guido, at the age of one, dies suddenly of meningitis.

1851	Throughout nearly the whole year Marx continues his economic studies with great intensity at the British Museum Reading Room. He fills some fourteen thick notebooks with excerpts. In April he believes he will shortly be able to conclude his researches and to start developing his great economic work. He negotiates with publishers. At the beginning of December Bonaparte's coup d'état and the resulting work on *The 18th Brumaire* causes an interruption. Throughout the year the London chapter of the League of Communists holds weekly meetings – with varying regularity – under Marx's chairmanship.
28 March 1851	Birth of Marx's daughter Franziska.
c. 5 August 1851	Marx is invited by Dana in New York to contribute to the *New York Daily Tribune*. On 8 August Marx requests Engels to send him an article, written in English, 'on the German conditions' and on 14 August he suggests that they should write 'a series of articles about Germany, from 1848 onwards'. On 21 August Engels sends Marx the first part of the series *Revolution and Counter-Revolution in Germany* and from then until 24 September 1852 he sends another eighteen articles of the series which appear in *Tribune* between 25 October 1851 and 23 October 1852 under Marx's name.
Late November 1851	Freiligrath informs Marx of Lassalle's plan to set up a limited company in Germany for the publication of Marx's economic writings. Marx declines because 'the bourgeois would not lend themselves to it at this moment' (after Bonaparte's coup d'état) and also because this plan might compromise him by disclosing his precarious financial situation.
Mid-January 1852	Marx instigates the founding of a new London German workers' association; he issues instructions for the drafting of its statutes.
14 April 1852	Marx's daughter Franziska dies at the age of one year.
Early September 1852	The Marx family in extreme trouble: Mrs Marx, Jenny, and Helene Demuth are sick, Marx has no money either for the doctor or for medicines, and is unable to write any articles for *Tribune* because he cannot buy any newspapers himself.
17 November 1852	The League of Communists declares itself dissolved on Marx's motion and declares its further existence in London as well as on the continent – where it had in fact ceased to exist since the arrest of the Cologne communists in May 1851 – as 'no longer meeting the requirements of the day'.

January 1853	After a break of about twelve months Marx resumes his economic studies. Various circumstances – sickness, journalistic work, etc. – soon divert him again and prevent him from resuming his work on economic theory until the end of 1856.
c. 20 April 1853	The *Revelations* are published in Boston as a special reprint from *Neu-England Zeitung* in a print run of about 500 copies.
	After a prolonged break Marx again receives a letter from Lassalle who asks him a favour in connection with Countess Hatzfeldt's lawsuit.
July–September 1854	Marx in great financial straits.
Late November 1854	Receives a proposition from Lassalle to work as a correspondent for the Breslau *Neue Oder-Zeitung*.
20 December 1854	Marx promises his collaboration to Moritz Elsner, the editor of the Breslau *Neue Oder-Zeitung*.
16 January 1855	Marx's daughter Eleanor is born.
6 April 1855	Marx's son Edgar dies.
Early March 1856	G. Levy reports to Marx a number of compromising facts about Lassalle's personal and political character; these are said to have given rise among the Düsseldorf workers to considerable outrage and hate of Lassalle. Marx's advice is that Lassalle should be 'watched' but that 'all public scandal should be avoided for the time being'. He discusses Lassalle's attitude, said to be giving rise to considerable mistrust, with Engels and W. Wolff.
22 May 1856	Mrs Marx with her three daughters travels to Trier to see her sick mother who dies on 23 July.
c. 1 October 1856	Marx moves into more spacious lodgings at 9 Grafton Terrace, Maitland Park, Haverstock Hill.
January–February 1857	In response to the news of an impending German translation of Proudhon's *Manuel du Spéculateur à là Bourse* Marx begins to write his Economy, beginning with a 'Chapter about Money'.
8 July 1857	Mrs Marx gives birth to a child which dies soon after.
4–10 June 1858	In a letter dated 4 June Lassalle gave Marx an extensive report on his duelling affair with Councillor Fabrice, requesting him to give him his 'exhaustive' opinion on the issue. Marx – having solicited Engels's and Wolff's views – explains in a letter dated 10 June that duelling is justified in certain cases where it is the only way for the individual to maintain himself against the one-sidedness and narrow-mindedness of bourgeois society, and, from the 'party point of view', approves of the rejection of the challenge in

the case in point as a deliberate gesture against the ceremonial of privileged classes.

c. 10 June 1859	*On the Critique of Political Economy. First Issue. By Karl Marx* is published in Berlin by the publishing house of Franz Duncker in 1,000 copies.
October–December 1859	Marx returns to his economic work. Embarks on new studies at the British Museum.
28 February–*c.* 14 March 1861	Short stay at Zalt-Bommel with his uncle Lion Philips, from whom he receives £160 as an advance against his share of the estate left by his mother.
c. 16 March–*c.* 13 April 1861	Marx in Berlin as Lassalle's guest. Discusses with him the possibility of founding a newspaper, without reaching any definitive result. In this connection Marx plans his Prussian re-naturalization and on 12 April gives Lassalle written authority to take whatever steps are necessary.
c. 19/20 April 1861	Marx visits his mother in Trier and stays for two days. His mother destroys some IOUs made out to her by Marx in the past.
Early June 1861	After a break of eighteen months Marx returns to his economic work.
c. 18 June 1861	Marx is informed by Countess Hatzfeldt that his re-naturalization application has been rejected by the Berlin Police President.
1862	Throughout the year Marx, with a few interruptions, works intensively on the draft of his economic work. About December he prepares a fair copy and decides to publish the entire work not as a continuation of *On the Critique* ... but as a separate book entitled *Das Kapital* and sub-titled *On the Critique of Political Economy.*
February 1862	Marx's daughter Jenny – driven by the family's desperate financial circumstances – attempts in vain, and without her parents' knowledge, to go on the stage.
9 July–4 August 1862	Lassalle stays in London; having arrived on 9 July to visit the Great Exhibition, he spends much time with Marx and his family.
January 1863	Marx starts preparing *Das Kapital* for press.
c. early June–12 June 1863	Marx receives from Lassalle his speech 'Indirect Taxation and the Situation of the Working Classes'; in a letter to Engels he criticizes this – as indeed Lassalle's political agitation generally – at considerable length and very sharply. He declares that he does not propose to take up a public position against Lassalle for the moment.

Mid-July–December 1863	About mid-July Marx gets down to the final editing and fair copying of *Das Kapital*. In the course of that work he considerably supplements and enlarges the available material. Added to this are new studies at the Reading Room and various interruptions, so that Marx does not finish the book until the end of 1865.
30 November 1863	Marx's mother dies in Trier.
c. 9–18 December 1863	Marx in Trier to settle his mother's estate.
21 December– 19 February 1864	Stay at Zalt-Bommel with his uncle, the executor of his mother's will. Marx falls ill there and remains until the end of February.
March 1864	Marx receives his share of the inheritance from Trier. He rents new accommodation at 1, Modena Villas, Maitland Park, Haverstock Hill.
3–19 May 1864	Stays in Manchester with Engels and the seriously-ill Wilhelm Wolff who dies on 9 May. Wolff leaves Marx £800.
1 September 1864	Freiligrath informs Marx that Lassalle has been wounded in a duel on 28 August.
2 September 1864	Marx receives from Freiligrath the news of Lassalle's death on 31 August.
	Liebknecht informs Marx that Schweitzer and other Lassalle followers, as indeed a great many workers, have proposed that Marx should come to Germany and assume direction of the General German Workers' Association. In a letter to Liebknecht of 12 September Marx declares that he is ready, on certain terms, to accept the presidency.
28 September 1864	From the speaker's platform at the assembly in St Martin's Hall, London, Marx attends the founding of an International Workers' Association. Marx is elected to the provisional committee as the representative of Germany.
16 October 1864	Marx declines Countess Hatzfeldt's request that he should write a tribute to Lassalle.
21–7 October 1864	Marx writes the inaugural address and the statutes of the International Association.
1 November 1864	Marx reads the address and the statutes to the committee, and these are unanimously adopted. The provisional committee constitutes itself as the Central Council.
3 November 1864	Marx meets Bakunin for the first time in sixteen years.
11 April 1865	At a sitting of the Central Council Marx is appointed Provisional Secretary for Belgium.
20 and 27 June 1865	At sittings of the Central Council Marx reads his lecture on wages, prices and profit.

Mid-November 1866	Marx sends the first sheets of *Das Kapital* to the publisher Meissner in Hamburg.
27 March 1867	Marx completes the fair copy of Volume I of *Das Kapital*.
3rd week of September 1867	Volume I of *Das Kapital* is published in a print run of 1,000.
1868	Marx is in continuous financial straits; he repeatedly considers moving to Geneva, where he could live much more cheaply; in the course of the year he receives approx. £400 from Engels.
2 April 1868	Civil wedding of Marx's daughter Laura to Paul Lafargue.
26 November 1868	Engels offers to pay all Marx's current debts and provide him with an annuity of £350 which would enable him to devote himself to his work undisturbed.
9 August 1869	Marx is invited by Max Friedländer to contribute again to the Vienna *Neue Freie Presse*.
	Liebknecht notifies Marx by telegram of the founding of the Social Democratic Workers' Party.
Early September– 11 October 1869	Marx travels to Aachen, Mainz, Siegburg, Hanover and Hamburg with his daughter Jenny.
c. 10–23 March 1870	Marx is again at work on *Das Kapital;* he has completed the first more or less finished revision of Volume II.
c. 18 September 1870	Engels moves to London, where he lives about ten minutes' distance from Marx. Henceforward Marx and Engels, with the exception of brief interruptions, due to journeys – meet almost daily until Marx's death.
c. 9–13 May 1871	Marx repeatedly meets a delegate of the Commune and sends instructions through him on 13 May.
Late May 1871	Marx completes his address on the Commune – *The Civil War in France* – and on 30 May reads it to the General Council; the address is adopted without discussion; at Engel's proposal it is resolved to have it printed in 1,000 copies.
28 June–29 July 1871	The address on the Commune, *The Civil War in France* is published in *Volksstaat* in Engels's German translation.
17–22 September 1871	Conference of the International Workers' Association in London, with Marx playing a prominent part and moving all the resolutions of the General Council.
December 1871	Marx starts on the revision of Volume I of *Das Kapital* for the second German edition.
5 March 1872	Marx submits to the General Council the confidential circular *Les Prétendues Scissions,* publication of which is unanimously agreed.
Early April 1872	Marx receives from Danielson a copy of the Russian translation of *Das Kapital* which was printed in 3,000 copies at

	the end of March and appeared in the bookshops on 9 April.
Early June 1872	The 'confidential circular' *Les Prétendues Scissions dans l'Internationale* is published in Geneva in 2,000 copies and is despatched to the sections.
1–7 September 1872	Fifth Congress of the International Workers' Association at The Hague, with Marx taking a very active part.
10 October 1872	Marx's daughter Jenny marries Charles Longuet.
January–April 1874	Marx processes a lot of material for Volume II of *Das Kapital*.
1 August 1874	Marx applies for naturalization to the British Home Secretary; his application is refused on 29 August on the grounds – withheld from Marx – that 'this man was not loyal to his own King and country'.
15 August 1874	Marx travels from London to Karlsbad with his daughter Eleanor.
19 August–21 September 1874	Sojourn in Karlsbad. Marx stays at the Hotel Germania on the Schlossberg.
18 March 1875	Engels writes to Bebel in his own and Marx's name about the issue of the merger of the Eisenach and Lassalle followers, and most sharply criticizes the draft programme; in the event of its being adopted by the Congress Marx and he would publicly dissociate themselves.
15 August–11 September 1875	Sojourn in Karlsbad. Marx stays at the Hotel Germania on the Schlossberg. Marx is placed under 'appropriate surveillance' by the Austrian police.
	Marx develops a detailed mathematical representation of the ratio between surplus value rate and profit rate ('Rate of Surplus Value and Profit Rate') for Volume III of *Das Kapital*.
15 August–15 September 1876	Sojourn in Karlsbad with Eleanor.
Late March 1877	Marx embarks on the revision of Volume II of *Das Kapital*.
8 August 1877	Marx travels to Neuenahr with his sick wife and Eleanor.
August 1877	Sojourn at Neuenahr. Marx under treatment by Dr Schmitz, who after a stay of three weeks advises convalescent treatment in the Black Forest both for him and his wife.
2–20 September 1877	Sojourn in the Black Forest.
February–April 1879	Mrs Marx seriously ill. Marx's own state of health deteriorates, so that at times he is totally incapable of work.

c. 8–15 August 1879	Marx travels to Jersey with his daughter Eleanor. His throat complaint gets worse although his general state of health improves.
15–20 August 1879	Marx moves to St Helier, which he abruptly leaves a few days later in order to go to Ramsgate – via London – where his daughter Jenny has given birth to a baby.
24 August–18 September 1879	Makes a good recovery in Ramsgate.
Late June 1880	Marx, who is in an advanced stage of exhaustion, is forbidden by his doctor to do any work for a protracted period. Because of his wife's progressing illness he is unable to travel to the continent to recuperate.
August–13 September 1880	Sojourn at Ramsgate with his wife, daughters and sons-in-law; Marx makes a good recovery.
Early October 1880	Marx requests Darwin in a letter to accept the dedication of Volume II of *Das Kapital*; Darwin declines, on the grounds – among others – that he does not wish to offend his family's religious sentiments.
February–June 1881	Marx suffers from chronic colds which disturb his sleep. He is forbidden all night work. His wife's condition deteriorates.
Late June–late July 1881	Marx with his sick wife at Eastbourne for recuperation.
26 July–16 August 1881	Marx with his wife visit their daughter Jenny in Argenteuil.
August 1881	Because of the high incidence of sickness in his family Marx again falls into debt. Engels helps him with £50.
c. 10–31 October 1881	Marx has peritonitis combined with bronchitis and incipient pneumonia. His life is in danger for several days. Mrs Marx has been bedridden since her return from Paris and daily becomes weaker.
2 December 1881	Mrs Jenny Marx dies of cancer of the liver after years of painful illness.
5 December 1881	Interment of Mrs Jenny Marx at Highgate, with Engels speaking at the graveside. Marx himself not permitted by his doctor to attend the funeral.
c. 1–16 January 1882	Marx with Eleanor at Ventnor.
20 February–2 May 1882	Sojourn in Algiers, where Marx arrives with peritonitis. He suffers from insomnia, loss of appetite and depression. Because of the exceptionally bad weather his general condition deteriorates.
2–7 May 1882	On the advice of Dr Stephann Marx travels via Marseilles (5 May) and Nice (5 and 6 May) to Monte Carlo, where he arrives on 7 May with renewed peritonitis.

8 June– 22 August 1882	Stay with Jenny Longuet at Argenteuil, where Helena Demuth and, since late July, Eleanor have also been staying. Marx makes daily visits to the sulphur baths of Enghien.
23–c. late August 1882	Marx and Laura Lafargue staying at Lausanne.
Late August– 18 September 1882	Marx and Laura Lafargue at Vevey, where he makes a good recovery.
Late September– early Ocrober 1882	Marx stays at Argenteuil for a few days en route back to London.
October 1882	Stays in London for about three weeks, then goes to Ventnor.
c. 3 November– 12 January 1883	Sojourn at Ventnor, where Marx contracts a series of new colds and is permanently confined to his room. Only sporadically capable of work.
Early January 1883	Nervous distress caused by the news of his daughter Jenny's serious illness results in a worsening of Marx's condition.
11 January 1883	Marx's daughter Jenny dies in Paris.
12 January 1883	At the news of the death of his daughter Jenny Marx returns to London.
Mid-January– February 1883	Marx has bronchitis and laryngitis which renders swallowing almost impossible.
February–14 March 1883	A tumour develops in Marx's lung; his bronchitis and laryngitis improve.
13 March 1883	Marx dies of his lung tumour towards 2.45 pm at his home at 41 Maitland Park Road.
17 March 1883	Marx is buried at Highgate Cemetery; Engels delivers the speech by the graveside.

Biographical Index

ALLEN, English physician, treated Marx and his family.

ARGOUT, ANTOINE-MAURICE-APOLLINAIRE, COMTE D', 1782–1858, French politician. Held various ministerial posts between 1830 and 1834. Chief Director of the Bank of France from 1834 to 1857.

ASSING, LUDMILLA, 1821–80, authoress. Friend of Lassalle.

BAKUNIN, MIKHAIL ALEKSANDROVICH, 1814–76, Russian officer of aristocratic origin. From 1840 in Germany. His friendship with Herwegh in Dresden (1842) resulted in contact with Young Hegelians and pre-revolution literature. 1848 participation in Dresden uprising, following its failure escaped with Richard Wagner. Repeatedly arrested, imprisoned (1851–60 in Russia), escaped (1860 from Siberia via Japan and America to London). Main theoretician of revolutionary anarchism and opponent of Marxism. Expelled from the First International in 1872.

BALZAC, HONORÉ DE, 1799–1850, French writer, recognized as the originator of the technique of the orthodox classical novel.

BAMBERGER, SIMON, London banker.

BANGYA, JANOS (JOHANN), 1817–68, Hungarian officer and journalist. In 1848/9 participated in the revolution in Hungary. In emigration an agent of the Austrian and/or French and Prussian police. Became a Turkish officer and press officer. Died as a Turkish police lieutenant.

BARROT, CAMILLE-HYACINTHE-ODILON, 1791–1873, French bourgeois politician. During the July monarchy leader of the liberal opposition. From December 1848 to October 1849 Premier.

BARTHÉLEMY, EMMANUEL, c. 1820–55, French worker, follower of Blanqui, member of revolutionary secret societies, participant in 1848 June uprising in Paris. One of the leaders of the Blanquist French emigré association in London. Executed in 1855 for a criminal offence.

BAUER, BRUNO, 1809–82, philosópher, religious historian and political writer. Young Hegelian. His Bible criticism was directed against the orthodox concept of the deity. After 1866 a national liberal. Contributor to *Kreuzzeitung*.

BAUER, EDGAR (brother of Bruno Bauer), 1820–86, political writer, Young Hegelian. From 1861 Prussian official.

BEBEL, AUGUST, 1840–1913, the most important leader of the German working-class movement. Trained as a cabinet-maker to whom in 1863, at the time of the foundation of Lassalle's 'General German Workers' Association' 'socialism and communism' were 'totally unfamiliar concepts, double-dutch words', in 1869, together with Wilhelm Liebknecht, in Eisenach founded the 'Socialist Workers' Party' whose unquestioned leader he remained, even after its merger, in Gotha in 1875, with the Lassalleans. His fiery parliamentary speeches – from 1868 he was continuously a member first of the North German and later the German Reichstag – are part of the history of German social democracy, as are also his books, above all his autobiography *From My Life*. Under his leadership social democracy at the time of the socialist legislation developed into the strongest party.

BECKER, HERMANN HEINRICH, 1820–85, County Court official and political writer in Cologne. 1848 member of the Cologne 'Democratic Society' and member of the executive of the 'Association for Workers and Employers'. 1849–50 editor of *West-deutsche Zeitung*. From 1850 member of the 'League of Communists'. 1852 sentenced in the Cologne communist trial. Later became national-liberal Mayor of Dortmund and Cologne.

BECKER, JOHANN PHILIPP, 1809–86, brush-maker. Participated in the democratic movement of the thirties and forties and in the 1848 revolution. Commander of the Baden Popular Guard during the Baden-Palatinate uprising of 1849. From 1848 communist. Later collaborator of Marx and Engels in the International Workers' Association. Co-founder of the Geneva section of the International and editor of the Geneva periodical *Der Vorbote*.

BERNARDIN DE ST PIERRE, JACQUES-HENRI, 1737–1814, French writer.

BERNAYS, KARL LUDWIG, 1815–79, radical journalist. Prior to 1843 on the staff of *Mannheimer Abendzeitung*, 1844 editor of the Paris *Vorwärts!* which was published with Marx's collaboration. In 1849 emigrated to the USA.

BERNSTEIN, EDUARD, 1850–1932, German socialist who gained intellectual prominence in 1896–8 through articles which criticized the rigidity of Marxist theory.

BERRYER, PIERRE-ANTOINE, 1790–1868, French lawyer and politician. Under the Second Republic Deputy of the Constituent and Legislative National Assemblies.

BISKAMP (BISCAMP), ELARD, democratic journalist. Participant in 1848–9 revolution. Emigrated to London and there in 1859 founded the emigré paper *Das Volk*, whose editorship Marx took over at a later date.

BISMARCH, OTTO VON, PRINCE, 1815–98, Prussian statesman who founded and became first chancellor of the German Empire.

BLANC, JEAN-JOSEPH-LOUIS, 1811–82, early socialist journalist and historian, 1848 member of the provisional government, afterwards emigrated to England. He rejected the idea of the class struggle, saw the 'State as the instrument for the liberation of the proletariat' and envisaged state-supported co-operative workshops.

BLANK, KARL EMIL, 1817–93. Merchant, brother-in-law of Friedrich Engels. In the forties and fifties gravitated towards socialist views.

BÖRNSTEIN, HEINRICH, 1805–92, Austrian revolutionary. Cut short an officer's career, became a journalist and actor. Founder of the Paris *Vorwärts* 1844. In 1849 went to USA. In St Louis, starting as an innkeeper, he became proprietor of a brewery, theatrical manager and publisher of *Anzeiger des Westens*. In the Civil War he fought on the Unionist side as Colonel of the 2nd German Missouri Regiment and was the principal leader of the insurrection of the Germans in St Louis. In 1863 President Lincoln sent him to Bremen as Consul.

BORKHEIM, SIGISMUND LUDWIG, 1825–85, journalist. Participant in 1848/9 revolution (storming of the Arsenal in Berlin and Baden-Palatinate uprisings). Emigrated via Switzerland and France to London, where in 1851 he settled as a merchant. From 1860 friendly with Marx and Engels.

BRADLAUGH, CHARLES, 1833–91, English journalist. Social reformer and opponent of socialism. After the Paris uprising of the Commune he attacked Marx and the International Workers' Association.

BRECHT, BERTOLT, 1898–1956, German poet, playwright and theatrical reformer.

BREYER, FRIEDRICH ALBERT, 1812–76, physician, liberal. In Brussels during the forties, there member of the 'Association Démocratique'.

BROCKHAUS, HEINRICH, 1804–74, publisher. From 1823 to his death head of the Leipzig publishing firm of F. A. Brockhaus.

BUCHER, LOTHAR, 1817–92, judiciary official, journalist. 1848 Deputy in the Prussian National Assembly (left centre). After the 1848/9 revolution emigrated to London. Contributed to Berlin *National-Zeitung*. Later close collaborator of Bismarck at the Prussian Foreign Office.

BÜHRING, KARL JOHANN, born 1820, worker. Member of the 'League of Communists'.

BÜRGERS, HEINRICH, 1820–78, radical journalist in Cologne. 1842/3 on staff of *Rheinische Zeitung*. 1848 member of the Cologne chapter of the 'League of Communists'. 1848/9 on editorial staff of *Neue Rheinische Zeitung*. 1850 member of the central authority of the 'League of Communists'. 1852 one of the principal defendants in the Cologne communists trial and sentenced to six years' imprisonment. Later national liberal.

BURNS, LYDIA (LIZZY), 1827–78, Irish working girl. Lived with her sister Mary and Friedrich Engels. Engels married her on her death-bed.

BURNS, MARY, died 1863, Irish working girl. From 1845 to her death lived, unmarried, with Friedrich Engels.

BURNS, MARY ELLEN (PUMPS), born c. 1860, niece of Lizzy Burns. From 1881 married to the merchant Percy Rosher.

CALDERÓN DE LA BARCA, PEDRO, 1600–81, Spanish poet.

CARNOT, LAZARE-NICHOLAS, 1753–1823, French scientist, politician and military expert. During the French Revolution first a Jacobin, later participant in the anti-Robespierre conspiracy of Ninth Thermidor. One of the organizers of the defence of France against the Coalition of European States.

CAUSSIDIÈRE, MARC, 1808–61, French socialist. In 1834 participated in the Lyons uprising. One of the organizers of revolutionary secret societies during the July monarchy. After the February revolution 1848 Police Prefect of Paris and Deputy of the Constituent National Assembly. Following the overthrow of the insurrection of June 1848 he emigrated to England.

CAVAIGNAC, LOUIS-EUGÈNE, 1802–57, French politician and general. Moderate republican. Participated in the conquest of Algeria in the thirties and forties and acquired notoriety for his barbarian warfare. 1848 Governor of Algiers. May–June 1848 Minister of War, smashed the Paris June uprising. Premier from June to December 1848.

CECILIA, see LA CECILIA, NAPOLEONE.

CHANGARNIER, NICOLAS-ANNE-THÉODULE, 1793–1877, French general and politician, monarchist. After the Paris June insurrection of 1848 commander-in-chief of the National Guard and the Paris garrison. After Louis Napoleon's coup d'état of 2 December 1851 was expelled from France.

CHATEAUBRIAND, FRANÇOIS-RENÉ, VICOMTE DE, 1768–1848, French writer, statesman and diplomat.

CICERO, MARCUS TULLIUS, 106–43 BC, Roman statesman, lawyer, orator and writer.

CLEMENT, KNUT JONG BOHN, 1803–73, historian and philologist. Professor at the University of Kiel.

CLUSS, ADOLF, c. 1820 – after 1889, engineer. Member of 'League of Communists'. 1848 secretary of the Workers' Educational Association in Mainz. 1849 emigrated to USA. Employed by Admiralty in Washington. Worked for German, English and American democratic journals. Political collaboration with Weydemeyer.

CONTZEN, KARL WILHELM, economist. Research fellow at the University of Leipzig.

COTTA, JOHANN GEORG, 1796–1863, publisher. From 1832 managed the Cotta publishing house in Stuttgart.

DANA, CHARLES ANDERSON, 1819–97, American journalist. Member of the Republican Party. Editor of the *New York Daily Tribune* and *New American Cyclopaedia*, to which Marx contributed.

DANIELS, ROLAND, 1819–55, Cologne physician. Member of the Cologne chapter of the 'League of Communists' (1850 member of the Cologne central authority). One of the defendants in the Cologne communists trial 1852, acquitted.

DANTON, GEORGES-JACQUES, 1759–94, orator and a leader of the French Revolution. Initially championed the extreme left but was executed when his calls for moderation seemed to threaten the extreme policies of the Revolutionary government.

DEMUTH, HELENE, 1823–90, from 1834 the Marx's family maid.

DERBY, EDWARD GEORGE GEOFFREY SMITH STANLEY (from 1851 Earl of Derby), 1799–1869, British statesman, three times Prime Minister.

DEUTSCH, SIMON, 1822–77, Austrian bibliographer. 1848 on the staff of the Vienna paper *Der Radikale*. Emigrated to Paris.

DIDEROT, DENIS, 1713–84, man of letters, philosopher and chief editor of the French *Encyclopédie*.

DILKE, ASHTON WENTWORTH, 1850–83, British politician, journalist and explorer. Newspaper publisher.

DISRAELI, BENJAMIN (from 1876 Earl of Beaconsfield), 1804–81, British statesman and writer. Prime Minister 1868 and 1874–80.

DONKIN, English physician. Treated Marx and his family 1881–3.

DÖNNIGES, HELENE VON, 1845–1911, daughter of the Bavarian Envoy to Switzerland. Engaged to the Rumanian nobleman Janko von Racowitza, who mortally wounded Lassalle in a duel in 1864.

DRONKE, ERNST, 1822–91, political writer. Initially a follower of 'true socialism', then member of the 'League of Communists'. 1848/9 one of the editors of *Neue Rheinische Zeitung*. Emigrated to Switzerland 1849, subsequently to England. Retired from political life in 1852.

DUNCKER, FRANZ GUSTAV, 1822–88, publisher. Representative of the German Progressive Party. One of the founders (with Max Hirsch) of the Hirsch-Duncker Trade Union Associations (1868), a merger of bourgeois-liberal trade unions which by December 1869 had 258 local associations with 30,000 members. Under Hirsch's leadership membership (1890) rose to 26 per cent of all free trade unions.

DUPIN, ANDRÉ-MARIE-JEAN-JACQUES, 1783–1865, French jurist and politician. President of the Legislative National Assembly 1849–51. Later follower of Napoleon III.

EBNER, HERMANN, journalist. During the eighteen-forties and -fifties secret agent of the Austrian police.

ECCARIUS, JOHANN GEORG, 1818–89, Thuringian tailor, member of the 'League of the Just', later of the 'League of Communists'. For many years an associate of Marx, jointly with him member of the General Council of the First International. In 1872, after quarrelling with him, he joined the English trade union movement.

EISERMANN, joiner, in the eighteen-forties a follower of Karl Grün, leading member of the 'League of the Just' in Paris.

ELSNER, KARL FRIEDRICH MONITZ, 1809–94, Silesian political writer and politician. 1848 Deputy of the Prussian National Assembly (left wing). In the fifties editor of *Neue Oder-Zeitung*.

ENGELS, ELISABETH FRANCISKA MAURITZIA, 1797–1873, mother of Friedrich Engels.

ENGELS, FRIEDRICH (SENIOR), 1796–1860, father of Friedrich Engels, a Pietist. Together with Ermen founded the cotton spinnery of Ermen & Engels in Manchester in 1837 and subsequently in Engelskirchen.

ENGELS, HERMANN, 1822–1905, brother of Friedrich Engels, manufacturer in Barmen.

ENGELS, MARIE, 1824–1901, sister of Friedrich Engels, married Karl Emil Blank in 1845.

ERMEN, GOTTFRIED, co-proprietor of the firm of Ermen & Engels in Manchester.

ERMEN, PETER (PITT), co-proprietor of the firm of Ermen & Engels in Manchester.

D'ESTER, KARL LUDWIG JOHANN, 1811–59, Cologne physician. Member of the Cologne chapter of the 'League of Communists'. 1848 member of the Pre-Parliament and one of the leaders of the Left in the Prussian National Assembly. Elected to the Central Executive of the Democrats of Germany at the 2nd Democratic Congress in Berlin October 1848. 1849 Deputy for the extreme Left in the Second Chamber.

Played an important part in the Baden-Palatinate uprising 1849 and subsequently emigrated to Switzerland.

EWERBECK, AUGUST HERMANN, 1816–60, physician and writer. Head of the Paris chapters of the 'League of the Just', later member of the 'League of Communists' which he left in 1850.

FAUCHER, JULIUS, 1820–78, political writer. Young Hegelian, champion of free trade. From 1850 to 1861 emigré in England. Following his return to Germany first member of the Progressive Party, from 1866 national liberal.

FERMÉ, French jurist, republican. Banished to Algiers during the Second Empire. Later judge of the Algiers State Tribunal. Acquainted with Charles Longuet and Paul Lafargue.

FEUERBACH, LUDWIG ANDREAS, 1804–72, German philosopher and theologian whose thought, with that of Hegel, particularly influenced the theories of Marx and Engels.

FLOCON, FERDINAND, 1800–66, French politician and political writer, bourgeois democrat. Editor of La Réforme. 1848 member of the provisional government.

FOX, PETER (real name Peter Fox André), died 1869, journalist. Participant in constituent assembly of the International Workers' Association. From 1865 official press correspondent of the General Council.

FREILIGRATH, FERDINAND, 1810–76, poet. His very first volume of poetry was so successful that the King of Prussia awarded him a pension (1842). But his next poems were already forbidden and F. turned revolutionary in the sense of the progressive bourgeoisie. He emigrated to Brussels, where he made Marx's acquaintance, and then to Zurich. After an intermediate stay in London F. in 1848 returned to Germany, and although remaining, as he put it, an 'emotional socialist', he became the most important poet of the bourgeois revolution. His poem 'The Dead to the Living' – as indeed many other published in Neue Rheinische Zeitung, on which F. worked as an editor – resulted in his arrest and detention. Emigrated to London 1851, returned to Germany 1868. In 1871 he wrote enthusiastic poems on victory but at the same time declined all official honours from the new German Empire.

FREUND, in the fifties the physician of the Marx family in London.

FRIEDLÄNDER, MAX, 1829–72, political writer, bourgeois democrat. On the editorial board of Neue Oder-Zeitung and the Vienna Presse to which Marx contributed in the fifties and sixties. Cousin of Ferdinand Lassalle.

FRIEDRICH WILHELM IV, 1795–1861, King of Prussia 1840–61.

GERSTENBERG, ISIDOR, London banker, follower of Gottfried Kinkel.

GOETHE, JOHANN WOLFGANG VON, 1749–1832, German writer.

GRANDPERRET, MICHEL-ÉTIENNE-ANTHELME-THEODORE, 1818–90, French politician. From 1867 Chief Public Prosecutor in Paris.

GRIMM, JACOB, 1785–1863, philologist and cultural historian. With his brother Wilhelm established Germanic studies as a linguistic and literary discipline. The two jointly published the first four volumes of the Deutsches Wörterbuch, the German Dictionary. By 'the Grimm method' Marx evidently means the method of preparation and publication of the dictionary: it appeared in separate issues, the different letters and/or words were processed independently of each other.

GRÜN, KARL, 1817–87, bourgeois democratic journalist. In the mid-thirties one of the principal representatives of 'true socialism', participant in the 1848/9 revolution; 1850 to 1862 in emigration. From 1870 in Vienna.

GUERRIER, French socialist, friend of Ewerbeck's, close to Marx and Engels in the forties.

GUIZOT, FRANÇOIS PIERRE GUILLAUME, 1787–1874, French historian and statesman. From 1840 to 1848 in charge of France's domestic and foreign policy.

GUMPERT, EDUARD, died 1893, German physician in Manchester.

HAIN, AUGUST, emigré in London. Member of the 'League of Communists'.

HARNEY, GEORGE JULIAN, 1817–97, influential English workers' leader, represented the left wing of the Chartists. Editor of various papers and periodicals. Member of the Brussels Communist Correspondence Committee, co-founder of the 'Fraternal Democrats'. Member of the First International. Lived in the USA from 1863–88.

HATZFELDT, EDMUND COUNT OF, 1798–1874, divorced by his wife for ill-treatment.

HATZFELDT, SOPHIE COUNTESS OF, 1805–81, friend of Ferdinand Lassalle who was her legal representative from the time of her divorce suit in 1846.

HECKER, FRIEDRICH FRANZ KARL, 1811–81, Mannheim lawyer, bourgeois democrat and republican. One of the leaders of the Baden uprising in April 1848. Thereafter emigrated to Switzerland, later to the USA. Participated in the Civil War as a colonel in the Unionist Army.

HEGEL, GEORG WILHELM FRIEDRICH, 1770–1831, German philosopher, whose Idealism can be said to have precipitated the social action of the Marxists.

HEINE, HEINRICH, 1797–1856, German poet and prose-writer.

HEINE, MATHILDE, 1815–83, wife of Heinrich Heine.

HEINZEN, KARL (Carl), 1809–80, radical political writer and bourgeois democrat. Participant in the Baden-Palatinate uprising 1849. Emigrated to Switzerland, then to England, and in the autumn of 1850 to the USA. There editor-in-chief of *Pionier*.

HERACLITUS (Greek: Herakleitos), c. 550–480 BC, philosopher from Ephesus. Even in antiquity called 'the Obscure' because of his cryptic language.

HERWEGH, GEORG, 1817–75, poet. Leading representative of German pre-revolution literature. After his expulsion from Tübingen Abbey (1836) worked on numerous pre-revolutionary and revolutionary periodicals, i.e. Gutzkow's *Telegraph für Deutschland* and Karl Marx's *Rheinische Zeitung*. In *21 Bogen aus der Schweiz*, published by himself in Switzerland (1843), which evaded the twenty-sheet clause of the German censorship, he published, among other things, Friedrich Engels's first major political polemic. During the Paris February revolution he was elected by the Germans to be President of their Republican Committee (of which Georg Weerth was also a member) and with a handful of armed men attempted to come to the aid of the Baden insurgents. Following the failure of the uprising he went into exile in Switzerland. As previously in Paris, so later in Switzerland, his house became the centre of the European revolutionary intelligentsia. After his return to Germany (1866) honorary correspondent of the First International.

HESS, MOSES, 1812–75, bourgeois democratic journalist and philosopher, one of

KARL MARX–FRIEDRICH ENGELS

the founders of 'true socialism'. Co-founder, editor and correspondent of *Rheinische Zeitung*. Member of the 'League of the Just', subsequently the 'League of Communists'. Emigrated to Paris in 1849 and remained there until his death. After 1846 in conflict with Marx and Engels; when the 'League of Communists' split up in 1850 he joined the Willich/Schapper wing; after 1863 follower of Lassalle; 1869 he turned towards the Social Democratic Workers' Party. Participated in two congresses of the International (1868 and 1869).

HOWELL, GEORGE, 1833–1919, bricklayer. One of the leaders of the British trade unions. Participated in the constituent assembly of the International Workers' Association.

IMANDT, PETER, schoolmaster in Krefeld, democrat. Participated in the 1848–9 revolution and after its defeat emigrated first to Switzerland and then to London. Member of the 'League of Communists'.

JONES, ERNEST CHARLES, 1819–69, English proletarian poet and political writer. Leader of the left wing of the Chartists. Co-editor of the *Northern Star*, editor of Chartist papers.

KAPODISTRIAS, JOHANNES COUNT, 1776–1831, Greek statesman and diplomat. From 1809 to 1822 in Russian service. President of Greece 1827–31. Victim of assassination.

KATKOV, MIKHAIL NIKIFOROVICH, 1818–87, reactionary Russian journalist.

KINKEL, JOHANN GOTTFRIED, 1815–82, poet and political writer. Bourgeois democrat, participated in Baden-Palatinate uprising 1849. Sentenced to life imprisonment, escaped to England with the help of Carl Schurz. One of the leaders of the bourgeois democratic emigrés in London.

KNILLE, OTTO, 1832–98, painter.

KOLLER, London publisher.

KOŚĆIUSZKO, TADEUSZ ANDRZEJ BONAWENTURA, 1746–1817, leader of the Polish national liberation movement during the seventeen-nineties.

KRAPÜLINSKI, Marx's nickname for Napoleon III. Properly the main character in Heinrich Heine's poem 'Two Knights', a Polish nobleman flinging his money about. The name is formed from the French word *crapule*, meaning gluttony (especially in drink) and lazy licentious rabble.

KUGELMANN, GERTRUD, wife of Ludwig Kugelmann.

KUGELMANN, LUDWIG, 1828–1902, Hanover physician, a friend of Karl Marx, with numerous contacts with German revolutionaries. Participated in the 1848 revolution. Member of the International. Greatly contributed to publicity for *Das Kapital* in Germany.

LA CECILIA, NAPOLEONE, 1835–78, Italian revolutionary. Participated in Garibaldi's campaigns in 1860 and 1861. Member of the Paris organization of the International Workers' Association. General of the Paris Commune; after its overthrow emigrated to England.

LAFARGUE, FRANÇOIS, died 1870 or 1871, father of Paul Lafargue.

LAFARGUE, PAUL, 1842–1911, physician, French socialist. One of the founders of the French workers' party 1879. Member of the First International (corresponding secretary for Spain 1866–8 and co-founder of the sections in France, Spain and Portugal). Son-in-law of Karl Marx (married to Marx's daughter Laura).

LASSALLE, FERDINAND, 1825–64, founder of the social-democratic movement in Germany. During the forties radical democrat. Contributed to *Neue Rheinische Zeitung*. 1849 sentenced to six months' imprisonment for incitement to sedition. In the fifties concerned himself chiefly with philosophical, historical and legal-philosophical studies. On behalf of the German workers' associations he drafted a programme which the General German Workers' Association (ADAV) adopted at its creation in Leipzig in 1863. Lassalle was elected president of this first social-democratic workers' party.

LAUTZ, Trier banker.

LEDRU-ROLLIN, ALEXANDRE-AUGUSTE, 1807–74, French political writer and politician. One of the leaders of the bourgeois democrats. Editor of the paper *La Réforme*. 1848 Minister of Interior of the provisional government. Emigrated to England 1849.

LENCHEN, see DEMUTH, HELENE.

LEVY (LEWY), GUSTAV, Düsseldorf paint manufacturer and merchant. Member of the 'League of Communists'. Friend and follower of Lassalle, co-founder and treasurer of the General German Workers' Association.

LIEBIG, JUSTUS VON, 1803–73, chemist. One of the founders of agricultural chemistry.

LIEBKNECHT, ERNESTINE, née Landolt, died 1867, first wife of Wilhelm Liebknecht.

LIEBKNECHT, WILHELM, 1826–1900, political writer. One of the leaders of the German working-class movement. Participant in 1848 revolution. Emigrated to Switzerland, then to England, there member of 'League of Communists'. 1862 return to Germany, and 1863–5 member of the General German Workers' Association. 1866 founder and leader of the Saxon People's Party which he – jointly with Auguste Bebel – represented as the first Deputy of a left-wing party in the North German Reichstag. 1869 co-founder of the Social-Democratic Workers' Party. Member of the German Reichstag 1874–1900. 'Responsible editor' of *Demokratisches Wochenblatt*, of *Volksstaat* and of *Vorwärts*. Father of Karl Liebknecht.

LORMIER, MARIE, friend of the Marx family.

LOUIS-PHILIPPE, 1773–1850, King of France 1830–48.

LÖWE, WILHELM, 1814–86, elected to the Frankfurt National Assembly by the Prussian Constituency of Calbe, who was punningly nicknamed 'der Löwe von Calbe', the 'Lion of Calbe'.

LUPUS, SEE WOLFF, WILHELM.

MADDISON, Scottish physician in London.

MAGENDIE, FRANÇOIS, 1783–1855, famous French physician and professor of medicine.

MARX, EDGAR (called Musch), 1847–55, son of Karl Marx.

MARX, ELEANOR (Tussy), 1855–98, youngest daughter of Karl Marx. Was active in the British and international working-class movement. From 1884 common law wife of Edward Aveling.

MARX, FRANZISKA, 1851–2, daughter of Karl Marx.

MARX, HEINRICH, 1782–1838, father of Karl Marx.

MARX, HEINRICH GUIDO, 1849–50, son of Karl Marx.

MARX, HENRIETTE, 1788–1863, mother of Karl Marx.

MARX, JENNY, *neé* von Westphalen, 1814–81, wife of Karl Marx. There were seven children of the marriage: Jenny, 1844–83; Laura, 1845–1911; Edgar (Musch), 1847–55; Heinrich Guido, 1849–50; Franziska, 1851–2; Eleanor, 1855–98; name unknown, 8 July 1857.

MARX, JENNY, 1844–83, eldest daughter of Karl Marx, journalist. Married Charles Longuet 1872.

MARX, LAURA, 1845–1911, second daughter of Karl Marx; married Paul Lafargue 1868. Was active in the French working-class movement.

MASSOL, MARIE-ALEXANDRE, 1805–75, French journalist. Friend of Proudhon.

MAZZINI, GIUSEPPE, 1805–72, Italian bourgeois democratic revolutionary. One of the leaders of the national liberation movement in Italy. 1849 head of the provisional government of the Roman Republic. 1850 one of the organizers of the 'Central Committee of European Democracy' in London.

MEISSNER, ALFRED, 1822–85, writer. Friend of Heine from 1847.

MEISSNER, OTTO KARL, 1819–1902, Hamburg publisher. Published *Das Kapital* and other works by Marx and Engels.

METAXAS, ANDREAS COUNT, *c.* 1786–1860, Greek statesman and diplomat. Premier 1843/4. From 1850–4 Minister to Constantinople.

MIALL, EDWARD, 1809–81, British politician and political writer. Leading representative of non-conformism. Member of Parliament in the fifties and seventies. Publisher of the *Non-Conformist* 1841–79.

MOLL, KARL JOSEPH, with Schapper developed the London Communist Correspondence Bureau from the 'League of the Just'.

MONROE, Dr, a Scot whose children Jenny Marx taught.

MOORE, SAMUEL, *c.* 1830–*c.* 1895, British jurist, judge in Manchester, legal adviser of Marx and Engels whose close personal friend he was. Member of the International. Translated the *Communist Manifesto* into English and likewise – jointly with Edward Aveling – the first volume of *Das Kapital*.

MÜLLER, WILHELM (pseudonym of Wolfgang Müller von Königswinter), 1816–73, poet, in the forties a Düsseldorf physician.

VON MÜLLER-TELLERING, EDUARD, fugitive member of the *Neue Rheinische Zeitung* staff.

NAPIER, SIR CHARLES, 1786–1860, British admiral, 1854 Commander-in-Chief of the Baltic fleet.

NAPOLEON I BONAPARTE, 1769–1821, Emperor of the French 1804–14 and 1815.

NAPOLEON III, LOUIS BONAPARTE, 1808–73, nephew of Napoleon I, President of the Second Republic from 1848–52, Emperor of the French from 1852–70.

NEUHAUS, physician from Thuringia, 1849 commanded a detachment of the Baden–Palatinate revolutionary army.

NICHOLAS I, 1796–1855, from 1825–55 Tsar of Russia.

O'CONNOR, FEARGUS EDWARD, 1794–1855, one of the leaders of the left wing of the Chartists. Founder and editor of *The Northern Star.*

OLMSTED, FREDERICK LAW, 1822–1903, American landscape gardener. Author of books on England and North America. Contributor to the New York *Putnam's Monthly Magazine* which in 1855 published Engels's series of articles *The Armies of Europe.*

OTTERBERG, W., bourgeois democrat, 1847 member of the German workers' association in Brussels.

OTTO I, 1815–67, Bavarian Prince, King of Greece 1832–62.

PALMERSTON, HENRY JOHN TEMPLE, VISCOUNT, 1784–1865, British statesman. Secretary of State for War, Foreign Affairs, Home Secretary, Prime Minister.

PATZKE, Chief of Berlin Police.

PHILIPS, JACQUES, Rotterdam lawyer. Cousin of Karl Marx.

PHILIPS, LION, died 1866, merchant of Zalt-Bommel. Uncle of Karl Marx. Executor of the will of Karl Marx's mother. The family was one of the founders of the Philips enterprises.

PIEPER, WILHELM, born c. 1826, philologist and journalist. Member of the 'League of Communists', emigré in London.

PINDAR, EDUARD, Russian emigré, lived in England about the middle of the nineteenth century.

PLANCK, GOTTLIEB, 1824–1910, jurist and politician. From 1867 national liberal member of the North German and German Reichstag and of the Prussian Chamber of Deputies.

PLATER, WLADISLAW, 1806–89, Polish politician. Participated in the 1830/1 uprising in what was then the Russian-controlled part of Poland. Subsequently emigrated.

POTTER, GEORGE, 1809–93, carpenter, British trade-union leader, founder and publisher of *The Bee-Hive Newspaper*, the mouthpiece of the International Workers' Association. 1870 broke off relations with the International Workers' Association for ideological reasons at Marx's instigation.

PROUDHON, PIERRE JOSEPH, 1809–65, French social philosopher and theoretical economist (came from a poor artisan background and worked as a typesetter). One of the theoretical founders of anarchism. The slogan 'property is theft' was coined by him, but he conceded property acquired by work. In his *Confessions*, translated by Arnold Ruge in 1850, he hoped to build a world between private property and common ownership. He justified anti-authoritarian attitudes, directed against both the state socialism of Louis Blanc and the communism of Cabet or indeed the Social Democratic Party. His attempt to set up a People's Bank (and to direct it), which very soon worked for 60,000 people, failed not for economic reasons but because of his sentence of three years' imprisonment for his attacks against Louis Bonaparte. Proudhon eventually – 'as a disinterested opponent' – turned against Marx whom, in his letter of defection in 1846, he warned against making himself the 'leader of a new intolerance', the 'apostle of a new religion', albeit one of logic or reason, against trying to sermonize or schoolmaster the people, and against operating with 'excommunication' and 'anathema'. An entry in his diary calls Marx the 'tapeworm of socialism', the all-devouring liquidator.

PÜTTMANN, HERMANN, 1811–94, poet and journalist. In the mid-forties one of the principal representatives of 'true socialism'. Emigrated to Australia after the 1848 revolution.

PUMPS, see BURNS, MARY ELLEN.

RAVEAUX, FRANZ, 1810–51, Cologne tobacco merchant. Bourgeois democrat, 1848/9 member of the Frankfurt National Assembly (left centre), Reich Envoy to Switzerland. 1849 member of the provisional Reich regency and of the Baden provisional government. Emigrated after the failure of the Baden-Palatinate uprising.

REINHARDT, RICHARD, 1829–98, poet. Emigré in Paris. Heinrich Heine's secretary.

RENSHAW, friend of Engels.

RICARDO, DAVID, 1772–1823, British economist, follower of Adam Smith and – as the writer rounding off classical bourgeois political economy – one of the most important precursors of Marx. His theories of money, ground rent and labour wage as well as his principal work *On the Principles of Political Economy and Taxation* were regarded by Marx as the most important preliminary studies for *Das Kapital*.

RICHELIEU, ARMAND-JEAN DU PLESSIS DUC DE, 1585–1642, French statesman. From 1622 Cardinal.

ROESGEN, CHARLES employee of the firm of Ermen & Engels in Manchester.

RÖSING, JOHANNES, born 1791, Bremen merchant. From 1848 directed the Democratic Association in Bremen.

RUGE, ARNOLD, 1802–80, Young Hegelian. Editor of *Hallische Jarbücher*, then published Marx's first really comprehensive political treatise. With Marx, Feuerbach and Bakunin founded the newspaper *Deutsch-Französische Jahrbücher* (*German–French Annals*). Broke with Marx in quarrel over Herwegh.

RÜSTOW, FRIEDRICH WILHELM, 1821–78, officer and military author, democrat. Participated in 1848/9 revolution. Emigrated to Switzerland. From 1860 participated in Italy's war of unification as Guiseppe Garibaldi's Chief of Staff. Friend of Lassalle.

SAINT-JUST, LOUIS-ANTOINE-LÉON DE, 1767–94, French revolutionary and apologist for the more extreme measures of the Revolutionary government.

SCHAPPER, KARL, with Moll ran the London Communist Correspondence Bureau.

SCHÖNBEIN, CHRISTIAN FRIEDRICH, 1799–1868, Swiss chemist. Founder of geochemistry.

SCHRAMM, CONRAD, c. 1822–58, political writer and publisher. Member of the 'League of Communists', participated in 1848/9 revolution. After 1849 emigré in London. 'Responsible editor' of *Neue Rheinische Zeitung. Politisch-ökonomische Revue*.

SCHWEITZER, JOHANN BAPTIST VON, 1834–75, Frankfurt lawyer and politician. One of Lassalle's closest collaborators. 1867–71 President of the General German Workers' Association. Publisher and editor-in-chief of *Social-Demokrat*. After 1871 retired from political life.

SEILER, SEBASTIAN, *c*. 1810–*c*. 1890, political writer. In the early forties in Switzerland a follower of Weitling. 1846 in Brussels he became a follower of Marx, a member of the Brussels Communist Correspondence Committee, subsequently the 'League of Communists'. 1848/9 in Paris, shorthand writer of the French National Assembly. Emigrated to New York 1856.

SELMNITZ, HUGO VON, Prussian officer. Acquaintance of Ferdinand Freiligrath.

SHELLEY, PERCY BYSSHE, 1792–1822, poet. Principal figure of the English romantic movement. In his writings opposed any kind of oppression.

SIEDEL, CARL, 1836–68, Rhineland poet. Distant relation to Engels. Contributed to the distribution of *Das Kapital* (Volume I) in Germany.

SIMON, JULES, 1814–96, French politician. One of the initiators of the struggle against the Paris Commune. 1876/7 Premier.

SMITH, ADAM, 1723–70, English economist. Regarded as the founder of classical English economics (main work: *Inquiry into the Nature and Causes of the Wealth of Nations*, 1776). Adam Smith first formulated the view that the value of goods was determined not by their user value but by their barter value. According to this concept the market price in the long run adjusts to the cost price – pre-supposing a free market economy. Adam Smith opposed state intervention (tariffs, import or export barriers, etc.). His theory of free trade was a major influence on economic policy in the late eighteenth and early nineteenth centuries. The source of wealth and social progress, to him, is the personal interest of the individual, man's natural urge to seek advantage.

SPIELMANN, London banker.

STEIN, JULIUS, 1813–83, Breslau headmaster, democratic political writer. 1848 Deputy of the Prussian National Assembly (left wing). In the fifties one of the editors of *Neue Oder-Zeitung*, after 1862 editor of *Breslauer Zeitung*.

STEPHANN, physician in Algiers, a native German.

STIEBEL, creditor of Karl Marx in London.

STOCKUM, VON, merchant from Düsseldorf. Count Hatzfeldt's man of affairs in his divorce suit.

STREIT, FEODOR, 1820–1904, lawyer, journalist and publisher, bourgeois democrat. During the 1848/9 revolution in Germany participated in the democratic movement.

STROHN, WILHELM, German emigré in Bradford. Member of the 'League of Communists'. Friend of Marx and Engels.

STRUVE, GUSTAVE, 1805–70, lawyer and political writer, bourgeois democrat. One of the leaders in the Baden uprisings in April and September 1848 and of the Baden–Palatinate uprising in 1849. Emigrated to England, where a leader of the bourgeois emigrés. Later went to the USA and participated in the Civil War on the side of the North.

SZEMERE, BERTALAN, 1812–69, Hungarian politician and political writer. During the 1848/9 Hungarian revolution Minister of the Interior and Head of the revolutionary government. Subsequently emigrated.

TAVERNIER, COUNT, artillery officer.

TAYLOR, TOM, 1817–80, English dramatist and journalist. Contributor to *Punch*.

THIERS, LOUIS-ADOLPHE, 1797–1877, French historian and statesman. 1832–4 repeatedly Minister, 1836 and 1840 Premier. After the February revolution on 1848 conservative republican. After Napoleon III's coup d'état 1851/2 exiled. After 1863 leader of the opposition against the Empire. 1871 crushed the Rising of the Commune. First President of the Third Republic from 1871–3.

TÜRR, ISTVÁN, 1825–1908, Hungarian general who deserted from the Austrian army to fight for the Piedmontese. Became governor of Naples.

TUSSY, see MARX, ELEANOR.

URQUHART, DAVID, 1805–77, British diplomat, political writer and politician. Member of Parliament 1847–52. Tory. Founder and editor of the periodical *Free Press* which was published in 1866 under the title *Diplomatic Review* (until 1877).

VINCKE, GEORG BARON VON, 1811–75, Prussian liberal politician. 1848/9 one of the leaders of the right wing of the Frankfurt National Assembly. In the fifties and sixties elected to the Chamber of Deputies of the Prussian Diet; moderate liberal.

VOGT, KARL, 1817–95, scientist, professor in Giessen. 1848 member of the Frankfurt National Assembly and 1849 member of the Provisional Reich Regency. Emigrated to Switzerland. Denounced to Marx as a bribed Bonapartist agent. When he publicly objected Marx replied to him in 1860 with the pamphlet *Herr Vogt*.

WALLAU, KARL, compositor on the *Deutsche Brüsseler Zeitung* which Engels claimed to have 'taken over', and original member of Marx's Communist Party founded in Brussels.

WATTS, JOHN, 1818–87, British political writer. Utopian socialist, later liberal.

WEERTH, Georg, 1822–56, German revolutionary writer. Member of the London centre of the 'League of Communists', (from 1843 in England), then 1845–7 in Brussels. From then on friendship with Marx, contributor to *Deutsche Brüsseler Zeitung*. 1848/9 literary editor of *Neue Rheinische Zeitung*. 1849 sentenced to three months' imprisonment for his 'Schnapphahnski'. Business trips (which were partly political courier journeys) through Holland, Spain, southern and central America (died in Cuba of tropical fever). Friedrich Engels called Weerth, who as a poet and critic had been greatly influenced by Heine, 'the first and most important poet of the German proletariat'.

WEITLING, WILHELM, 1808–71, tailor, for years one of the leading lights of the central agency of the 'League of the Just'. Original member of the Communist Party started by Marx in Brussels. His ideology gradually alienated Marx, whom he eventually criticized in a newspaper founded in New York, *Republik der Arbeiter* (*Workers' Republic*).

WESTON, JOHN, carpenter, later entrepreneur. Participant in constituent assembly of International Workers' Association. Member of its General Council from 1864 to 1872.

WESTPHALEN, EDGAR VON, 1819–c. 1890, brother-in-law of Karl Marx (brother of Jenny Marx). 1846 member of the Brussels Communist Correspondence Committee.

WESTPHALEN, HEINRICH GEORG VON, 1768–1855, uncle of Jenny Marx.

WESTPHALEN, KAROLINE VON, died 1856, mother of Jenny Marx.

WESTPHALEN, LOUISE VON, 1805–61, wife of the Prussian Minister of the Interior, Ferdinand von Westphalen.

WEYDEMEYER, JOSEPH, 1818–66, German (later American) revolutionary democrat. Mid-forties influenced by 'true socialism', from *c.* 1846 supporter of Marxist views. Member of the 'League of Communists' (1849–51 head of its Frankfurt chapter). Participated in 1848 revolution, one of the 'responsible editors' of *Neue Deutsche Zeitung* 1849/50. Emigrated to USA 1851, colonel in the Unionist Army in the Civil War.

WILHELM I, 1797–1888, Prince of Prussia. From 1858–61 Prince Regent; 1861–88 King of Prussia; 1871–88 German Emperor.

WILLICH, AUGUSTE, 1810–78, former Prussian lieutenant. Left the army because of his political convictions. Member of the 'League of Communists'. 1849 leader of a Free Corps in the Baden-Palatinate uprising. 1850, when the 'League of Communists' split, he was, together with Schapper, the leader of the anti-Marx grouping. Emigrated to USA 1853, there a Unionist general in the Civil War.

WOLF(F), FERDINAND, (the 'red wolf'; the 'Red') 1812–95, journalist. 1846/7 member of the Brussels Communist Correspondence Committee. Member of the 'League of Communists'. 1848/9 one of the editors of *Neue Rheinische Zeitung.* Emigrated to Paris and London. After the split of the 'League of Communists' in 1850 belonged to the pro-Marx grouping. Later retired from political life.

WOLFF, WILHELM (LUPUS), 1809–64, Silesian schoolmaster, from 1831 active as a radical student organization member, for which imprisoned 1834–8. From 1846 in Brussels, when his close friendship with Marx and Engels started. Active in the Brussels Communist Correspondence Committee. Member of the 'League of the Just', co-founder of the 'League of Communists', from 1848 in its central authority 1848/9 one of the editors of *Neue Rheinische Zeitung.* Member of the Frankfurt National Assembly (extreme left). Emigrated to Switzerland 1849, to England 1851. Wolff left Marx a substantial fortune. Marx dedicated the first volume of *Das Kapital* to him.

WURM, GUSTAV, 1819–88, philologist, early friend of Engels.

YORCK, THEODOR, 1830–75, joiner, co-founder of Social Democratic Workers' Party and one of its leaders.

ZABEL, FRIEDRICH, 1802–73, liberal political writer. Editor of the Berlin *National Zeitung.*

ZEDLITZ-NEUKIRCH, KONSTANTIN BARON VON, born 1813, Prussian civil servant, Police President of Berlin.

Chronological table and index of names compiled by Wilhelm Busch.

Index